MEETING THE CHALLENGE OF ADOLESCENT LITERACY

MEETING THE CHALLENGE OF ADOLESCENT LITERACY

Research We Have, Research We Need

Edited by

MARK W. CONLEY
JOSEPH R. FREIDHOFF
MICHAEL B. SHERRY
STEVEN FORBES TUCKEY

THE GUILFORD PRESS
New York   London

© 2008 The Guilford Press
A Division of Guilford Publications, Inc.
72 Spring Street, New York, NY 10012
www.guilford.com

Printed in the United States of America

This book is printed on acid-free paper.

Last digit is print number: 9 8 7 6 5 4 3 2 1

Library of Congress Cataloging-in-Publication Data

Meeting the challenge of adolescent literacy : research we have, research we need /
edited by Mark W. Conley ... [et al.].
    p. cm.
  Includes bibliographical references and index.
  ISBN-13: 978-1-59385-702-8 (pbk.)
  ISBN-13: 978-1-59385-703-5 (hardcover)
  1. Reading (Secondary)—United States.   2. Developmental reading—United States.
  I. Conley, Mark William.
  LB1632.M384 2008
  428.4071′2—dc22

                                                            2007042845

About the Editors

Mark W. Conley, PhD, is a professor and coordinator of the undergraduate and graduate Literacy Programs in the Department of Teacher Education at Michigan State University. His research focuses on literacy assessment, content-area literacy, and literacy policy. He is the author of *Connecting Standards and Assessment through Literacy* and *Content Area Literacy: Learners in Context.*

Joseph R. Freidhoff, BA, is a doctoral candidate in the Educational Psychology and Educational Technologies Program at Michigan State University. His areas of research include new literacy practices of preservice teachers, teacher collaboration and community, and teaching and learning in online environments. He currently teaches an elective course to help preservice teachers design technology-rich projects to implement during their internship year.

Michael B. Sherry, MEd, is a doctoral candidate in Michigan State University's Department of Teacher Education. A former middle and high school literature and drama teacher, he earned a master's degree in curriculum and teaching from Michigan State University while teaching abroad in a French international school. Back in the United States, he studies preservice English language arts teachers' decision-making processes, particularly how they learn to make improvisational, responsive decisions.

Steven Forbes Tuckey, MEd, is a doctoral candidate at Michigan State University. His research focuses on science and mathematics curriculum design, responsive pedagogy, technology and writing in the sciences, and history and philosophy of science and mathematics. These research interests emerge from his extensive experience within secondary and postsecondary classrooms teaching science, mathematics, and teacher education.

Contributors

Charles Anderson, PhD, Department of Teacher Education, College of Education, Michigan State University, East Lansing, Michigan

Mark W. Conley, PhD, Department of Teacher Education, College of Education, Michigan State University, East Lansing, Michigan

Gay Fawcett, PhD, independent consultant, Akron, Ohio

Joseph R. Freidhoff, BA, Department of Teacher Education, College of Education, Michigan State University, East Lansing, Michigan

Kristine Gritter, PhD, School of Education, Seattle Pacific University, Seattle, Washington

Amanda Hawkins, MA, Department of Teacher Education, College of Education, Michigan State University, East Lansing, Michigan

Kathleen A. Hinchman, PhD, Reading and Language Arts, Syracuse University, Syracuse, New York

Elizabeth Birr Moje, PhD, School of Education, University of Michigan, Ann Arbor, Michigan

Timothy Rasinski, PhD, Department of Teaching, Leadership, and Curriculum Studies, Kent State University, Kent, Ohio

Cathy M. Roller, PhD, International Reading Association, Newark, Delaware

Jon R. Star, PhD, Graduate School of Education, Harvard University, Cambridge, Massachusetts

Sharon Strickland, MEd, Department of Teacher Education, College of Education, Michigan State University, East Lansing, Michigan

Alfred W. Tatum, PhD, Department of Curriculum and Instruction, University of Illinois at Chicago, Chicago, Illinois

Steven Forbes Tuckey, MEd, Department of Teacher Education, College of Education, Michigan State University, East Lansing, Michigan

Deborah Vriend Van Duinen, MA, Department of Curriculum, Teaching and Educational Policy, Michigan State University, East Lansing, Michigan

Preface

Following in the tradition of *Shaping Literacy Achievement: Research We Have, Research We Need* (Pressley, Billman, Perry, Reffitt, & Reynolds, 2007), this volume synthesizes research in the area of secondary literacy. The chapters expand on presentations at the second annual conference of the Literacy Achievement Research Center at Michigan State University in the fall of 2006. Whereas the previous volume provided a more general overview of the terrain of literacy research, this book sets it sights more specifically on the population of adolescents and their literacies. Drawing on experts from diverse disciplines, the chapter authors present a perspective on the research we have and the research we need. While each chapter can stand alone, together they represent some of the preoccupying issues of the area. One such issue that is present throughout the chapters is the difference between elementary and secondary youth and their literacy practices. Another is the difference in perspectives between literacy researchers and researchers who study secondary content areas like math and science. Still another difference is the need to expand our conceptions of literacy and "text" while still allowing for dialogue among researchers and educators about successful instruction within disciplines. An overarching tension exists between the goals of validating adolescents' identities, their prior knowledge, and their out-of-school literacies, while at the same time helping them to connect, modify, and expand these practices to align with the literacy content, skills, and disciplinary practices of secondary content areas.

In Chapter 1, "Fluency for Adolescent Readers: The Research We Have, the Research We Need," Timothy Rasinski and Gay Fawcett address the problem of an increase in expectations and accountability for adolescent readers whose classes now focus on content, rather than on reading skills. The research we have suggests that one potential solution to this problem may be instruction in fluency: "the ability of readers to read quickly, effortlessly, and with good meaningful expression." Beginning with the influential National Reading Panel report (2000), which named fluency as one of five critical factors in reading development, Rasinski and Fawcett summarize the results, the controversy about, and the limitations of fluency research. The research we need, they suggest, should examine fluency instruction in relation to the training of teachers, to technology, and to independent reading.

Chapter 2, "Intervening When Older Youths Struggle with Reading: Teach Me What I Need to Know Next," written by Kathleen A. Hinchman, begins by recognizing the uniqueness and richness of adolescent literacy practices and stressing the interconnectedness of these practices with the formation of youths' multiple identities. In this chapter, Hinchman helps readers understand older youths' struggles with reading, using large-scale studies to quantify the problem, but also delving into factors that contribute to or present obstacles for dealing with this problem. Importantly, the chapter moves beyond locating and substantiating the problem to exploring research on the strategies teachers use for assessing older readers who struggle and the interventions teachers and students employ to improve youths' decoding strategies, fluencies, and vocabulary and comprehension knowledge. In an important contribution, Hinchman also draws upon her experiences working with struggling readers in a literacy clinic to expose the holes in the current research base, to validate the challenges teachers face when trying to personalize reading instruction to meet the needs of individual students, and to suggest future areas for research.

Alfred W. Tatum, in Chapter 3, "The Literacy Development of African American Male Adolescents: The Influence of Contexts and Texts," questions why African American adolescent males from poor communities continue to underperform in reading as assessed by standardized measures. The research we have, writes Tatum, is both scarce and limited, focusing more on at-risk factors than aspects of their racialized and gendered identities, and ignoring their coping skills. Examining how in- and out-of-school contexts and text selection influence the identity construction of these young men may be part of the answer. In a case study, Tatum used attention to the history of positive enabling texts for African American males to work with Quincy, a 16-year-old African American adolescent male from inner-city Chicago. The research we need, he suggests, must describe who these young men are, perhaps taking (as he does) a cultural–ecological stance that examines the inter-action of culture, context, and gender. More controlled, large-scale studies of schools with African American adolescent males are needed to complement suggested best practices, to aid in text selection, and to avoid essentializing.

Though recognizing that teachers need to make connections be-tween students' out-of-school backgrounds and experiences and the cur-riculum of schools, Elizabeth Birr Moje argues that responsive literacy teaching still needs to be accountable to the literacies of the disciplines. In Chapter 4, "Responsive Literacy Teaching in Secondary School Content Areas," Moje outlines three forms of knowledge that responsive literacy demands: (1) knowledge of youth, (2) knowledge of the disciplines, and (3) knowledge of the texts and literacy practices that both youth and the disciplines privilege. For each of these areas, she reviews the extant research, critiques the value of what we have, and recommends further development in each area. Additionally, to move the field forward, Moje argues that more research is needed to understand how preservice and inservice teachers learn to enact responsive pedagogies.

Making a detailed survey of current research in Chapter 5, "Strat-egies That Improve Adolescents' Performance with Content-Area Texts," Mark W. Conley, Joseph R. Freidhoff, Kristine Gritter, and Deborah Vriend Van Duinen examine the ways in which adolescents go about comprehending content-area texts. Through detailed analysis of jour-nals in different subfields of educational research, as well as web and database searches, the authors provide an enlightening view of the re-search we have—from interventions in whole-classroom settings to the struggles of adolescent readers to the complexities of online environ-ments. By distinguishing the skills and tactics used by adolescents in comprehending texts (strategies) from the pedagogical choices that teachers make in helping to foster them in students, this chapter allows for a more nuanced take on the surprisingly scarce corpus of research on the topic. As a result of their inquiry within these areas, the authors provide a coherent vision for future research on strategies for adolescent readers within specific contexts. They close their chapter with a call for research to address three important strands, all of which are present throughout other chapters in this book: further problematizing of "struggling readers" both in classrooms and beyond the boundaries of school; helping teachers make better use of literacy and disciplinary tools and models; and helping to improve student literacy in both general and subject-specific ways. Such research would broaden the vision of scholarship on literacy and provide greater space for thought and action.

In Chapter 6, "What Is Mathematical Literacy?: Exploring the Relationship between Content-Area Literacy and Content Learning in Middle and High School Mathematics," Jon R. Star, Sharon Strickland, and Amanda Hawkins—all mathematics educators—provide a discussion of "content-area literacy" from the perspective of those within the mathematics content area. Making use of their status as "literacy outsiders, but content insiders," they craft and discuss a compelling alternative (content-area *numeracy*) that provides a powerful critique of current content-area literacy policy and practice. They challenge the notion that, by attaching the term "literacy" to a content area, the ability to employ and discuss the new term (e.g., "mathematical literacy") is somehow unproblematic, regardless of the particularities of the content area. Moreover, by ignoring these content-related particularities, an exclusionary dichotomy (*literacy learning* vs. *content-area learning*) is generated for practitioners. Star and colleagues suggest that this forces educators into making an unproductive choice between *either* mathematics learning goals *or* literacy goals.

Steven Forbes Tuckey and Charles Anderson contribute Chapter 7, "Literacy in Science: Using Agency in the Material World to Expand the Conversation," which complements Star and colleagues' chapter by addressing the problem of differing conceptions of literacy—in this case, in relation to science literacy. Understanding commonalities and differences among scholarly traditions, in particular a common focus on encouraging "agency," may allow researchers and educators to collaborate with each other and also to assist secondary students more effectively. Using some commonplaces across traditions, the authors illustrate the differences between three perspectives that are part of the research we have on science literacy: content oriented, strategies oriented, and discourse oriented. Through a fictionalized encounter between a preservice teacher, Jennifer, and her student, Juan, they set each of these perspectives in motion. Having highlighted differences, Tuckey and Anderson show how these three traditions overlap and how current research is blurring their boundaries: all three have the common goals of increasing agency and understanding the situation of particular students. Finally, they suggest that the research we need must bring a similarly multifaceted perspective to the training of science teachers (a project they have begun through videocase work) in order to help educators make use of the affordances of all three traditions.

In the final chapter, "Literacy Coaching," Cathy M. Roller, the Director of Research and Policy at the International Reading Association, provides a detailed account of the ways in which literacy coaching is being researched and implemented. Citing many studies and ongoing projects, Roller provides us with a snapshot of where literacy coaches sit within the literature as they become more common in practice. In her analysis of recent studies on literacy and reading coaches, most of which are qualitative and highly contextual, she echoes the findings of Guskey (2000) by summarizing that "local, site-specific, instructionally focused, ongoing professional development generally works better than the traditional pull-out models focused on schoolwide or districtwide issues." Looking ahead to the research we still need, she calls for increased clarity on the definition of reading/literacy coaches and a more focused examination of the potential benefits that reading/literacy coaching could have for student achievement.

We believe that this volume will be a valuable asset to researchers, teacher educators, and teachers alike. It arrives at a time of unprecedented policy and change directed toward adolescent literacy.

MARK W. CONLEY
JOSEPH R. FREIDHOFF
MICHAEL B. SHERRY
STEVEN FORBES TUCKEY

REFERENCES

Guskey, T. R. (2000). *Evaluating professional development.* Thousand Oaks, CA: Corwin Press.

National Reading Panel. (2000). *Report of the National Reading Panel: Teaching children to read.* Washington, DC: U.S. Department of Health and Human Services, National Institutes of Health.

Pressley, M., Billman, A. K., Perry, K. H., Reffitt, K. E., & Reynolds, J. M. (Eds.). (2007). *Shaping literacy achievement: Research we have, research we need.* New York: Guilford Press.

Contents

1

Fluency for Adolescent Readers

The Research We Have, the Research We Need

TIMOTHY RASINSKI
GAY FAWCETT

It happens in classrooms around the country every day. Tens of thousands of middle school and high school teachers give assignments that require reading and hundreds of thousands of students don't do them. For many of the students, perhaps the majority, it is not out of rebellion or laziness. It is out of frustration and hopelessness. Is it any wonder when students who struggle with reading year after year finally give up?

THE PROBLEM

"Over the last twenty years America's public schools have heroically responded to a rising flood of expectations" (Vollmer, 2000) while the school day and the school year have remained virtually the same. These expectations have placed an increased demand on the reading skills of adolescents. Even in this age of technology, textbooks are the primary resource in most middle school and high school classrooms. As the demand for higher level skills has increased, so has the nature and difficulty of the textbooks. Core vocabulary accounts for a smaller portion of words in instructional texts than it did several decades ago (Hiebert,

2002). In addition, students are faced with more words than numbers in math books; more charts and graphs in social studies and science books; and more technical reading in computer classes and online. Some students who were successful readers in the primary grades suddenly flounder when they encounter the challenges of secondary textbooks.

Along with the push for higher standards, *accountability by acronym* has emerged: NCLB (No Child Left Behind), HQT (highly qualified teachers), RTI (response to intervention), AYP (adequate yearly progress), SI (school improvement), not to mention FCAT, OGT, SAT, TAKS, SOL, MEAP, NAEP, and MCAS (to name just a few of the multitude of high-stakes tests). This accountability has shone a light on reading problems because in addition to multiple-choice questions, nearly every state test now includes extended reading passages, regardless of the subject area.

It is evident that middle school and high school students more than ever before need to be better readers. Unfortunately, the problem is compounded by the fact that most secondary teachers see themselves *as content* teachers, not *reading* teachers, and therefore students often do not get the reading help they need to meet the rising flood of expectations and accountability. Most often help comes in the form of comprehension strategies. We would certainly never downplay the importance of comprehension instruction; however, we believe that there is another skill that deserves more attention than it is currently getting, both in the research and in middle school and high school classrooms: reading fluency.

What Is Reading Fluency?

"Reading fluency refers to the ability of readers to read quickly, effortlessly, and with good, meaningful expression" (Rasinski, 2003, p. 26). *Quickly* is not synonymous with *fast* in fluent reading. Fluent readers know when to speed up and when to slow down for effect. They know how to use the tone of their voices to help the passage come alive with meaning; they know when their voices should go up and when their voices should go down. They know how to chunk words into phrases and how to pause at punctuation. They automatically recognize words so that their reading can go on smoothly and without apparent effort.

Fluent reading allows readers to reserve their limited cognitive resources for the more important task in reading: comprehension (LaBerge & Samuels, 1970). There are currently two primary theories about how fluency contributes to comprehension. One theory maintains that automaticity in decoding and word recognition allows the reader to read fluently and thus construct meaning from the text. When automaticity is lacking, students literally exhaust their cognitive resources by investing so much of their mental energy in the decoding aspect of reading.

The other theory focuses on prosody (stress, pitch, phrasing, pausing, expression, and rate) as the primary contributor to comprehension. Proponents of this theory maintain that monotonal, staccato, and unenthusiastic reading renders the text difficult to understand.

Both notions of fluency seem valid and point to areas of instruction for teachers and investigation for researchers. For the purposes of this chapter, we include an integration of automaticity and prosody into our definition of fluency.

Where Does Fluency Instruction Belong?

From the earliest days of oral "round robin reading" until today fluency instruction has been associated with the elementary grades, and usually the primary grades. Fluency requires basic skills such as decoding, word recognition, and expression, which are taught in depth with beginning readers. Although few in number, fluency programs developed for classrooms have traditionally targeted the elementary grades (Chall, 1996; Rasinski, Padak, Linek, & Sturtevant, 1994; Stahl & Huebach, 2005). By the time students reach middle school, and certainly by the time they enter high school, teachers expect them to already know how to decode, to have a large stock of words they automatically recognize, and to read with expression. However, evidence is mounting that fluency instruction is as important for adolescent readers as it is for beginning readers, particularly for those who struggle with reading.

RESEARCH WE HAVE

National Reading Panel

Until recently reading fluency was not an area of widespread interest for the literacy community (Allington, 1982; National Reading Panel, 2000). Then, in 2000, the report of the National Reading Panel thrust fluency into the spotlight of reading instruction and research. The panel identified fluency as one of five factors, proven by empirical research, to be *critical* to students' overall reading development.

Members of the panel reviewed 14 immediate effects studies, 16 group learning studies, 12 single-subject learning studies, and nine method analysis studies. The immediate effects studies looked at the impact of repeated oral reading with feedback on improvement. All 14 studies, involving a total of 473 students in grades one through college, found improvements in word recognition, accuracy, rate, and comprehension.

The 16 group learning studies also focused on the effects of oral reading practice on other reading skills. These studies involved a total of 752 students in grades two through nine. Subjects in 11 of the studies were poor readers and subjects in the remaining five studies were average readers. In all but one study students demonstrated clear improvements in fluency, comprehension, word recognition, and overall reading skill.

In the 12 single-subject design studies, there were between two and 13 students per study. All of the subjects had some kind of learning problem (e.g., special education, learning disabilities, disfluent reading, below-grade-level skills, autism). The studies examined the impact of one-on-one tutoring or repeated reading. All but one study reported clear and substantial improvement in accuracy, speed, and comprehension. The panel reported that the one study that did not show student improvement had a weak design.

In reviewing the nine method analysis studies the panel was attempting to determine the efficacy of various oral reading strategies, including repeated reading with and without feedback, guided repeated reading, assisted nonrepetitive reading, and various peer or parent procedures that involved reading together. For the most part, the procedures were comparable. However, the panel concluded that there was not enough data to allow for a definitive conclusion.

In summary, the National Reading Panel found that fluency instruction has an impact on the reading ability of all readers at least through grade four, as well as on students with reading problems throughout high school. "If children read out loud with speed, accuracy, and proper expression, they are more likely to comprehend and remember the material than if they read with difficulty and in an inefficient way" (Teaching Children to Read, n.d.). The panel concluded that attention to fluency is appropriate for all ages.

Research Not Included in the National Reading Panel Review

One aspect of the National Reading Panel's report that generated a great deal of discussion and controversy was the panel's position on the role of independent reading in improving reading achievement. The panel reported that research does not show that an increase in the quantity of reading has a beneficial effect on reading achievement.

In contrast, many fluency experts maintain that Stanovich's (1986) classic article on the "Matthew effect" applies to fluency gained through independent reading. There is a line in the biblical Gospel of Matthew that says "For unto every one that hath shall be given, and he shall have abundance: but from him that hath not shall be taken away even that which he hath" (25:29). This line has often been paraphrased as "The rich get richer, and the poor get poorer." Applied to fluency, the Matthew effect would simply state: "The more one reads, the better reader one becomes. The less one reads, the farther behind one gets." Thus, the argument goes, programs such as SSR (Sustained Silent Reading) and DEAR (Drop Everything and Read) improve fluency, and therefore comprehension.

Allington (1977), in his article "If They Don't Read Much, How They Ever Gonna Get Good?," found that students who struggled most in reading spent the least amount of time in actual reading. In 1984 he reiterated this claim through research he conducted in a first-grade classroom where he found as few as 16 words were read in a week by children in a low-reading group compared to 1,933 words for children in a high-reading group.

Other researchers have reported similar findings. Biemiller (1977–1978) reported substantial ability-group differences related to how much reading students did. Nagy and Anderson (1984) found that good readers often read 10 times as many words as poor readers in a given school year.

In conclusion, while some fluency researchers lay claim to studies supporting the use of independent reading to increase fluency, there is division among the ranks on this issue.

National Assessment of Educational Progress

In 1995 the National Assessment of Educational Progress, sponsored by the U.S. Department of Education, commissioned a study of the status of reading fluency in U.S. education (Pinnell et al., 1995). The researchers found that fluency, whether measured in terms of automaticity or prosody, was strongly associated with silent reading comprehension for fourth-grade students. Alarmingly, 44% of the 1,000-plus, nationally representative sample of fourth graders in this study lacked even a minimal level of fluency, even with grade-level passages they had read under supportive testing conditions. A recent replication of the study, 10 years later (Dane, Campbell, Grigg, Goodman, & Orange, 2005), found much the same results: Reading fluency is significantly related to overall reading achievement for students beyond the primary grades and a significant number of these students lack even basic reading fluency skills.

Other Related Research

Rasinski and Padak (1998) found that among struggling elementary students (grades one through five) referred for Title I supplementary reading instruction by their regular classroom teachers, the lack of reading fluency appeared to be the area of greatest need. In Kent State University's reading clinic, difficulties in reading fluency are manifested in a majority of grades two through eight students who are referred for reading intervention. Although comprehension is the primary reason cited for most referrals (especially among intermediate and middle-grade students), fluency invariably accompanies the difficulties in comprehension.

A recent study (Rasinski et al., 2005) examined fluency among a large group of ninth-grade students in an urban school. Students in this district have historically performed poorly on the Ohio Graduation Test, which is given in grade 10. While word recognition accuracy was strong for most students (average decoding accuracy was 97.4%), over 60% of students in the sample read below the 25th percentile on fluency norms developed for eighth graders (as established by Johns & Berglund, 2002). More than 12% percent of the students assessed read less than 100 words per minute, a rate normally associated with primary grade readers. It is likely that poor scores on the test were a result of disfluent reading, which drained cognitive resources away from where they were needed most: comprehension of content.

More recently, working with school personnel from a large urban school district, Timothy Rasinski and Nancy Padak (2006) examined the results of informal reading inventories (IRI) administered in the fall to 76 ninth-grade students who were enrolled in schools identified as low performing. Again, although accuracy in word recognition was strong (94.5%), fluency as measured by words read correctly per minute (109) was, on average, poor. Students were reading at a rate that would be expected of second and third graders (using norms from Hasbrouk & Tindale, 1992). The students were also measured for prosody or intonation using a four-point scale developed by Pinnell and colleagues (1995) in their study of fourth-grade students. Of the 76 students, 44 (58%) received scores of 1 or 2 on a four-point scale, indicating they were not able to read with a minimal level of expression that reflected meaning making in their reading.

Research Conclusions

These studies along with others hold the promise that gains in fluency could account for significant gains in comprehension. We cannot say conclusively that disfluent reading causes poor comprehension; there are certainly other contributing factors such as inadequate background knowledge, insufficient vocabulary, or lack of reading strategies. Obviously, there is still much to be done in fluency research.

RESEARCH LIMITATIONS

There are a number of limitations to the research studies reported above. Each study has its own limitations. However, a composite list of limitations could include:

- Small sample size
- Lack of statistical power (due to small sample size)
- Unrepresentative sample
- Lack of control for variability within treated samples
- Lack of multivariate analysis to control for contextual variables
- Lack of replication
- Lack of random assignment

Perhaps the greatest dilemma facing researchers is the issue of correlation versus causation. The controversial conclusion of the National Reading Panel (2000) on the importance of frequent and sustained reading was made because the studies were all correlational studies. The panel reported:

> Although correlational findings may be useful, they also can be deceptive because correlations tell nothing about the direction or sequence of a relationship. That good readers read more could be because reading practice contributes to reading attainment, but it could also be simply that better readers choose to read more because they are good at it. If this is true, then it is reading achievement that stimulates reading practice, not the reverse . . . such studies do not permit a clear delineation of what is antecedent and what is consequent. (National Reading Panel, 2000, p. 3-10)

Developing fluency research studies to address the correlation/causation issue is complex and controversial in its own right. Withholding treatment from some students so that random assignment can be made is often an ethical and logistical struggle that is not easily resolved.

Due to the limitations listed above, caution in generalizing the results of the cited research studies is warranted.

RESEARCH WE NEED

The fluency research we have to date is promising and warrants more time and attention from teachers and researchers. The current research needs to be supplemented with additional studies involving more students, especially adolescents, in more contexts, over more time, and with more rigor. The research community needs to involve teachers in action research conducted in authentic classroom contexts.

We need to understand if technology enhances, interferes with, or has no effect on reading fluency. As with the review of independent reading, the National Reading Panel (2000) stated that research on the value of computer technology in reading instruction was too limited to allow conclusions. What are the effects of speech-supplemented computer text, hypertext, and Internet literacy?

Teacher inservice and preservice for adolescent readers rarely addresses fluency. What training yields results for students? What training formats work best? What kind of follow-up is necessary to keep newly learned fluency strategies alive in the classroom?

More research is especially needed to understand the influences that independent silent reading practices have on reading fluency. We also need additional research on the effects of fluency strategies such as repeated reading, paired reading, choral reading, and independent reading specifically on adolescent readers.

CONCLUSION

"Young people do more reading and writing today—on paper and online—than ever before. This means their literacy development is just as important, and requires just as much attention, as that of beginning readers" (Focus on Adolescent Literacy, 2006). The research to date is clear. Fluency instruction improves reading comprehension for adolescent readers. In this age of expectations and accountability, we owe it to our students to gather more evidence that will help us to help them even more.

REFERENCES

Allington, R. L. (1977). If they don't read much, how they ever gonna get good? *Journal of Reading, 21,* 57–61.

Allington, R. L. (1982). Fluency: The neglected goal of the reading program. *Reading Teacher, 36,* 556–561.

Biemiller, A. (1977–1978). Relationships between oral reading rates for letters, words, and simple text in the development of reading achievement. *Reading Research Quarterly, 13,* 223–253.

Chall, J. S. (1996). *Stages of reading development* (2nd ed.). Fort Worth, TX: Harcourt Brace.

Dane, M. C., Campbell, J. R., Grigg, W. S., Goodman, M. J., & Oranje, A. (2005). *Fourth-grade students reading aloud: NAEP 2002 special study of oral reading.* Washington, DC: U.S. Department of Education, Institute of Education Sciences.

Focus on Adolescent Literacy: IRA Programs and Resources. (2006). Newark, DE: International Reading Association. Retrieved October 30, 2007, from *www.reading.org/resources/issues/focus_adolescent.htm*

Hasbrouck, J. E., & Tindale, G. (1992). Curriculum-based oral reading fluency norms for students in grades 2 through 5. *Teaching Exceptional Children, 24,* 41–44.

Hiebert, E. (2002, November). *On the matter of text in fluency instruction and assessment.* Paper presented at the meeting of the Pacific Regional Educational Laboratory on A Focus on Fluency, San Francisco.

Johns, J., & Berglund, R. (2002). *Fluency: Questions, answers, evidence-based strategies.* Dubuque, IA: Kendall Hunt.

LaBerge, D., & Samuels, S. A. (1974). Toward a theory of automatic information processing in reading. *Cognitive Psychology, 6,* 293–323.

Nagy, W., & Anderson, R. C. (1984). How many words are there in printed school English? *Reading Research Quarterly, 19,* 304–330.

National Reading Panel. (2000). *Report of the National Reading Panel: Teaching children to read. Report of the subgroups.* Washington, DC: U.S. Department of Health and Human Services, National Institutes of Health.

Pinnell, G. S., Pikulski, J. J., Wixson, K. K., Campbell, J. R., Gough, P. B., & Beatty, A. S. (1995). *Listening to children read aloud.* Washington, DC: U.S. Department of Education, Office of Educational Research and Improvement.

Rasinski, T. V. (2003). *The fluent reader: Oral reading strategies for building word recognition, fluency, and comprehension.* New York: Scholastic.

Rasinski, T. V., & Padak, N. D. (1998). How elementary students referred for compensatory reading instruction perform on school-based measures of word recognition, fluency, and comprehension. *Reading Psychology; An International Quarterly, 19,* 185–216.

Rasinski, T. V., & Padak, N. D. (2006). Fluency beyond the primary grades: Helping adolescent struggling readers. *Voices from the Middle, 13,* 34–41.

Rasinski, T. V., Padak, N. D., Linek, W. L., & Sturtevant, E. (1994). Effects of fluency development on urban second-grade readers. *Journal of Educational Research, 87,* 158–165.

Rasinski, T. V., Padak, N. D., McKeon, C., Krug-Wilfong, L., Friedauer, J., & Heim, P. (2005). Is reading fluency a key for successful high school reading? *Journal of Adolescent and Adult Literature, 49,* 22–27.

Stahl, S., & Heubach, K. (2005). Fluency-oriented reading instruction. *Journal of Literacy Research, 37,* 25–60.

Stanovich, K. (1986). Mathew effects in reading: Some consequences of individual differences in the acquisition of literacy. *Reading Research Quarterly, 22,* 360–406.

Teaching Children to Read. (n.d.). Rockville, MD: National Reading Panel. Retrieved October 30, 2007, from *www.nationalreadingpanel.org/default.htm*

Vollmer, J. (2000). *The burden.* Retrieved October 30, 2007, from *www.jamievollmer.com/burden.html*

2

Intervening When Older Youths Struggle with Reading

Teach Me What I Need to Know Next

KATHLEEN A. HINCHMAN

Parents and grandparents approach me annually, at the start of our university's literacy clinic, quoting sons and daughters who have returned to us for an additional summer of tutoring: "Literacy clinic is the only place I go where they teach me what I need to know next." Many years of hearing such comments, and the youth's excitement about new learning at the end of our sessions, have led me to the conclusion that older youth who struggle with reading can benefit from literacy instruction—despite research suggesting that interventions for older youths have not been generally effective (Allington, 1994).

Other research suggests that older youths who face literacy-related academic challenges come to these with existing interests, understandings, strategies, and needs (Alvermann, 2001). Young people who appear to be illiterate in school often deploy effective out-of-school communication strategies—but will do so only in front of peers or family. Other youths—not many—struggle with reading in virtually all contexts. Youths in both groups need empathy, knowledge, perseverance, and instruction. Providing appropriate interventions that "teach me what I need to know next" is a complex endeavor at best: Allington

11

and Walmsley's (1995) admonishment that there is no quick fix is even more true for older youth who bring varying personal and instructional backgrounds to their struggles with reading.

This chapter is constructed from the stance that we have a moral obligation toward older youths who struggle with reading. More specifically, the purpose of the chapter is to review what sociocultural and cognitive research suggests about interventions for these individuals. It also explores what we don't know and need to know—about acknowledging youths' existing abilities and desires, about combining interventions to yield desired outcomes, and about designing programs to suit individuals' needs.

RESEARCH WE HAVE ON OLDER YOUTHS WHO STRUGGLE WITH READING

Adolescence *Is* a Real World

As Lesko (2001) observed, U.S. society's notions of *adolescence* connote pulsing hormones and individuals without responsibility who will be harshly awakened at adulthood, as in "When you're in the real world." Yet young people usually find that constructing identity is more complex than the preceding generalities suggest. In addition to school attendance and homework, some older youths take care of siblings or grandparents, or translate for non-English-speaking parents. Informed by background, means, and desires, they hold part- or full-time jobs, participate in extracurricular activities, or engage in projects with friends for hours after school. They confront relationship problems; learning disabilities; pregnancies; drug; alcohol, or physical abuse; eating disorders; or hunger, all of which send them messages about who they are, how they are valued, and to what they should aspire.

Literacies In and Out of School

Much research conducted since the mid-1990s has explored older youths' literacy enactments in and out of school. Beginning with a notion that literacy is socially situated (Gee, 1996; Street, 1995), such research has helped us to understand that, by the time they reach their teenage years, older youths develop multiple literacies suited to a variety of real and virtual contexts (New London Group, 1996). Such literacy practices may include graffiti writing, tagging (Moje, 2000), gaming

(Leander & Lovvorn, 2006), and reading (Finders, 1997) and producing 'zines, fanfictions, anime, and other publications (Blackburn, 2003; Chandler-Olcott & Mahar, 2003; Knobel, 2002; Lewis & Fabos, 2005).

Research has also described youths' acquisition of the subject-specific discourses needed for academic success (Lemke, 1990), noting that some youths are better positioned via home discourses for such acquisition (Gee, 2006). For instance, Hynds (1997) realized that youths found middle school English instruction more engaging when it allowed them to acknowledge personal life complexities. Hinchman and Zalewski (2001) discovered that youths in Zalewski's high school global studies class might benefit from added opportunities to explore and use social studies-specific language in their classroom work. More recently, Leander (2001) explored youths' management of multiple discourses as they enacted identity, agency, and power relations during a school field trip. Moje and her colleagues (2004) helped youths build on existing funds of knowledge to conduct experiments, shaping and being shaped by academic discourses as they worked. Hull and Schultz (2001) explained the blurriness in lines between out-of-school and in-school literacies, and argued that well-orchestrated instruction can help build bridges among these.

Literacy and Identity Construction

Donna Alvermann (2001) described Grady, a young man who struggled with school reading in ways that negatively affected his perception of himself. Yet when Grady was invited to explore out-of-school video game interests, he became the master to Alvermann's graduate assistant's apprentice—successfully reading to move to a next game level and teaching adults as he worked. Alvermann reasonably suggested that Grady could transfer such out-of-school literacies—and more positive identity construction—to school literacy tasks.

In a research study that considered identity constructions connected to one student, Leander (2002) showed how identity becomes stabilized when youths relate multiple, varied identity artifacts, including those generated in classroom discussions and literacy activities, as well as those produced in peer, home, and other social spaces. Like Grady, most young people who struggle with school literacy tasks engage in personal literacy practices that contribute some sense of ability to their identity. Yet some individuals struggle with decoding or print comprehension in ways that inhibit their overall feelings of competence. Such important aspects of identity construction must be taken into account in the design of instructional contexts in which such youths will more likely flourish.

How Many Older Youths Struggle with Reading?

The National Research Council recommended that schools employ well-trained specialists to work with students who struggle with reading (Snow, Burns, & Griffin, 1998). Quatroche and her colleagues noted that U.S. schools are employing fewer and fewer such specialists, which would seem to indicate that fewer older youths have been demonstrating significant difficulties with literacy (Quatroche, Bean, & Hamilton, 2001). However, the following statistics suggest that this is not the case.

National Assessment of Educational Progress

On the 2005 U.S. National Assessment of Educational Progress (NAEP), 64% of fourth graders and 73% of eighth graders and 12th graders performed at basic reading levels, while 31% of fourth graders and eighth graders and 35% of 12th graders reached proficiency. According to the NAEP, those reading at basic levels demonstrate only partial mastery of the knowledge and skills needed for success at a particular grade, while performance at proficiency suggests subject matter knowledge and skills appropriate for a particular grade. Average NAEP scores at both grades four and eight are a bit higher in 2005 than they were in 1992, but scores at grade 12 are lower. Scores indicate that a significant number of young people have difficulty with even very basic reading tasks, and that the performance of black and Hispanic youth continues to be lower than the performance of white youth (National Center for Educational Statistics, 2006, 2007).

More people stay in school longer than in previous generations, meaning that a more varied sampling of individuals is now tested than ever before (Allington, 2002). In addition, since no accommodations for special education students were allowed prior to 1998, those thought to be unable to take NAEP tests without such help were exempted from testing (National Center for Educational Statistics, 2007). This changed as a result of the reauthorizations, in 1997, of the Individuals with Disabilities Act (IDEA) and, in 2002, of the Elementary and Secondary Education Act, known as No Child Left Behind, which now require accountability for all students in state and federal assessment systems and allow for such accommodations as extended time on tests. This change means that we are less likely to lose youths in the system than we were in earlier decades—although this ruling too is fraught with frustration when youth are suddenly asked to take reading tests for which they have not been prepared (Thurlow & Wiley, 2006).

What Instruction Is Available?

Youths who struggle with reading and who are identified for special education receive widely varying instruction. Some attend subject-area classes and receive help to complete assignments or modified assignments. Because emphasis is usually placed on subject-area study, or because students who are frustrated in widely varying ways are grouped together, such students are likely to receive inadequate literacy instruction (Brasseur, Gilroy, & Schumaker, 2004)—despite the fact that intervention research suggests that many could learn to read at least at average levels with the right instruction (Vellutino & Scanlon, 2002).

Older youths who struggle with reading but who are not identified for special education may fair even worse, given the dearth of reading specialists beyond grade three. The National Reading Panel (2000) noted that competent one-to-one tutoring best addresses such needs, yet most schools cannot afford such an expense. Such instruction is usually provided to small or large groups of students, and is only sometimes provided by a trained reading specialist. Some schools ask an English teacher with limited understanding of literacy instruction to provide intervention. In a grotesque twist of the adage "every teacher a teacher of reading" (Moore, Readence, & Rickelman, 1983), other schools expect subject-area teachers with even more limited training to help struggling readers in their classes, disadvantaging subject-specific teaching and literacy instruction.

How Assessment Helps

"Monitoring student progress" and "data-driven instruction" are buzz phrases in schools that worry about students' reading development (Marzano, Pickering, & McTighe, 1993). Monitoring can be generated from teachers' complaints about youths who cannot or will not engage in subject-area reading assignments. Monitoring students' reading also often begins when NCLB-mandated assessments yield results that do not meet federal standards for adequate yearly progress. Low performance by subpopulations of English language learners or individuals of a particular ethnic, gender, special education, or socioeconomic status are also cause for alarm in U.S. schools given current government regulations for disaggregated data reporting.

Screening Tests

Statewide assessment of reading comprehension uses grade-appropriate texts with multiple-choice and sometimes essay questions. They gauge the comparative success of youths in schools, districts, and states, screening for those who struggle; they do not tell about youths' reading strategies or ability to read or write in the various contexts needed for success following school. School districts that are especially concerned with test scores may purchase additional assessment systems to monitor students' progress with added frequency, sometimes using such curriculum-based measurement tools as Dynamic Indicators of Basic Early Literacy Skills (DIBELS; Good & Kaminski, 1996), even though the predictive validity of such oral reading assessment is unclear, especially at higher grade levels (Pressley, Hilden, & Shanklin, 2006). Schools also often require teachers to drill students in preparation for such tests. All such activities take time away from instruction that may be more suited to youths' interests and future needs (Afflerbach, 2004).

Low performance by an individual student on a statewide or an all-school screening test means that the individual is targeted for intervention services or, possibly, not promoted to the next grade. Intervention planning then begins with an analysis of the student's test answers to discern error patterns for follow-up instruction. Because the screening snapshot is taken at 10,000 feet, this picture overlooks strengths youths demonstrate in more familiar contexts (Jones, Carr, & Ataya, 2006). Scores also mask variability, and youths with longer school histories exhibit remarkably varied profiles (Buly & Valencia, 2002) that are better investigated with collaborative, less formal observation tools, interest inventories, and instructional interactions.

Informal Reading Inventories

Informal reading inventories (IRIs) can be used to learn about some of a youth's reading strengths and needs. These informal tools also help a teacher estimate the degree of text complexity with which a youth is most comfortable, depending on prior knowledge and interest. An IRI requires that a student reads aloud passages from a variety of texts while a teacher notes and, later, analyzes the student's oral reading miscues (Johnson & Kress, 1965). IRIs can be completed with any available text, gathered to test a teacher and student's hypotheses over time. Teachers can also use published IRIs whose passages are organized according to text readability, structure, or content (e.g., Leslie & Caldwell, 2005), although their relatively short passages may not align well with a youth's day-to-day or future reading requirements (Paris & Carpenter, 2003).

With some variation, both informal and published IRIs tend to use criteria to determine reading levels that are similar to those delineated long ago by Betts. Betts (1950) and others recommended counting the number of miscues per 100 words, noting rate, expression, and comprehension to discern a reader's independent, instructional, and frustration levels relative to the reading of particular texts. In this view, a text is estimated to be at a reader's instructional level when about 90–94% of words are read accurately, with about 75% comprehension. Readers who reach these percentages are thought to have ability to construct meaning with similar texts, especially when a teacher can explain and model needed strategies.

Patterns of miscues hint of areas for instruction. Goodman, Watson, and Burke (1987) suggested analysis of semantic, syntactic, and graphophonic aspects of miscues. Does the misread word make sense in context? Is it the right part of speech? What letter cues does the reader use? Does the reader misread certain parts of words, such as middle syllables or endings? Does the reader substitute visually similar words? Is the reader skipping words or lines? Is the reader able to retell the content of text read aloud, or to answer questions following reading? One might also notice a reader's general fluency, rate, and expressiveness.

Think-Alouds

Word-level and comprehension strategies can be understood better when teachers ask students to talk about what they're doing as they read and write (Van Someren, Barnard, & Sandberg, 1994). Youths can think aloud about the workings of their reading during informal reading inventories—although in our clinic we've observed that this can be a confusing dual-purposed task. Alternatively, Goodman and Marek (1996) invite older youths to listen to recordings of their reading. They are then invited to collaborate with a teacher to discern and address miscue patterns (Wilson, 2005).

Assessing Word Analysis Strategies

To gain a more detailed sense of youths' approaches to figuring out unknown words, a teacher can ask them to read aloud graded lists of words, such as the San Diego Quick Assessment (Ekwall & Shanker, 1999). Many teachers use the spelling assessment described by Donald Bear and his colleagues (Bear, Invernizzi, Templeton, & Johnston, 2003). Organized to assess knowledge of developmental spelling patterns, this assessment can help a teacher design instruction based on a more nuanced understanding of youths' letter–sound insights.

Intervention Designs

Extra reading instruction was once called "remedial." However, this term has been widely critiqued for creating limited expectations and motivation (Johnston & Allington, 1991). The term "early intervention" was introduced to describe programs meant to catch young people up with their peers before they lost motivation (Clay, 1993). The term "intervention" is now used to represent any program intended to accelerate progress for those who struggle with reading (Greenleaf, Jiménez, & Roller, 2002).

Types of Interventions

Vellutino and Scanlon (2002) explain that early interventions vary widely, describing three categories meant to prevent long-term reading difficulties:

- Text-emphasis approaches, such as Reading Recovery (Clay, 1993), which help children to develop metacognitive strategies to comprehend and write stories.
- Code-oriented approaches, such as Phonological Awareness Plus Synthetic Phonics (Torgesen, Wagner, & Rashotte, 1999), emphasize explicit phoneme awareness and phonics instruction.
- Combined approaches, such as Modified Reading Recovery (Iversen & Tunmer, 1993) and the Interactive Strategies Approach (Vellutino & Scanlon, 2002), teach metacognitive strategies for reading and writing, combined with structured activities to teach decoding skills and strategies.

Lessons in all three categories include interactive reading, writing, and skills and strategies development, varying in focus and amount of time spent. It is interesting that this combination of activities mirrors the categories of instruction recommended by Betts (1950) in an instructional framework used in many published reading programs over the last half century, including recent balanced literacy frameworks (Pressley, 2006).

Interventions for Older Youths

Studies of literacy or reading intervention beyond grade five are limited but reflect the same patterns as can be found in emergent literacy interventions, although no empirical reason can be given for choosing one pattern over another when working with an individual older youth. For example, Gaskins, Gaskins, and Anderson (1995) found that code-emphasis decoding by analogy instruction helped older youths improve their word reading, spelling, vocabulary, and comprehension. Similarly, Bhattacharya and Ehri (2004) found that graphosyllabic instruction helped older youths to pronounce and spell words. In a meaning-emphasis approach, Jiménez (1997) used culturally relevant texts in two languages to teach bilingual middle-grade youths to draw on their existing language abilities to determine word meanings, questions, and inferences. In an additional meaning-based approach, O'Brien (2003) successfully invited youths to design Internet-based multimedia inquiry projects on their own topics. Diamond, Corrin, and Levinson (2004) created a successful meaning-based intervention for ninth graders with increased instructional time, explicit comprehension instruction using challenging and engaging material, and strong teacher–student relationships. Similar patterns are reflected in long-used adult literacy tutoring models that are sometimes used with older youth, such as Proliteracy Worldwide's code-emphasis *Laubach Way to Reading* (Laubach, Kirk, & Laubach, 1981) and meaning-emphasis *Tutor* (Cheatham, Colvin, & Laminack, 1993).

What to Teach

Much research over the last 20 years has focused on providing explicit instruction to develop the declarative, procedural, and conditional knowledge needed for proficient reading (Paris, Lipson, & Wixson, 1983). Instruction that explains the nature of procedural strategies, and conditions of their use, has long focused on the development of reading comprehension strategies (Duke & Pearson, 2002). However, strategic approaches to other aspects of reading have also recently been described, as when Vellutino and Scanlon (2002) suggested that we use word-level strategies to decode, and Graves (2006) noted that we use word-learning strategies to develop vocabulary knowledge.

Strategy instruction depends on teacher explanation and modeling of needed strategies, either organized around the systematic teaching of strategies or, more incidentally, with strategies taught as needed for reading (Duke & Pearson, 2002; Graves, 2006). Teachers encourage gradual release of responsibility when they invite youths to engage in guided and, eventually, independent practice (Pearson & Gallagher, 1983). Teachers and youths can collaborate on using such strategies in increasingly integrated fashion in increasingly complex, varied texts, including those needed for academic success.

Developing Strategic Decoding

In an attempt to help older youths to notice and pronounce medial graphic detail in words, Bhattacharya and Ehri (2004) conducted a study comparing graphosyllabic analysis with whole-word reading and no special instruction. Youths in the treatment group spent 4 days segmenting a large number of multisyllabic words, using only the rule that one has a separate syllable for each vowel sound, flexibly assigning adjacent consonants to one syllable or the other, and blending segmented syllables together to reform the whole word. Syllable-trained youths' posttest results were superior to the results of both other groups, suggesting that such a strategy may be useful to older readers, confirming similar work by Shefelbine and colleagues (Shefelbine, 1990; Shefelbine & Calhoun, 1991; Shefelbine, Lipscomb, & Hern, 1989).

Bear and his colleagues (2003) described stages of word knowledge for youths who have learned to read and have begun to make richer, meaning-based connections for spelling in syllable patterns and affixes, and in other derivational relations. They suggest how older youths can study consonant and vowel patterns in multisyllabic words; how syllables join together; how stress affects sounds; how affixes change usage, meaning, and spelling; and how base word parts evoke almost the same meanings in multiple words that vary only by affix (e.g., *current/occurrence, bibliography/telegraph*). They recommend word study notebooks and word sorts, use in context, and meaning inquiry to learn such aspects of words.

Developing Strategic Fluency

"Fluency" refers to readers' ability to read with a rate and connectedness that supports sense making. This includes prosody, or phrasing and expressiveness, skills that reflect insights about the coupling of syntax with meaning. Some readers struggle with fluency because they do not have effective decoding strategies, while others can decode but struggle with putting words together into meaningful, connected reading (Rasinski & Padak, 2006).

Readers' fluency is likely to improve with independent reading of a variety of texts (Biancarosa & Snow, 2004; National Reading Panel, 2000). In addition, the most often recommended instructional method for improving oral reading fluency involves repeated oral reading (Samuels, 1979). Students are asked to reread bits of text until they can be read aloud fluently, and to understand that this strategy can be used whenever oral reading is demanded. Teacher-assisted repeated reading involves instruction, modeling, and mimicking in phrasing and expression, and is described by Kuhn and Stahl (2003) as being even more effective than simple repeated reading.

Developing Strategic Vocabulary Knowledge

The relationship between vocabulary knowledge and reading comprehension has long been examined in the research literature. Graves and Watts-Taffe (2002) note that vocabulary knowledge is tied to verbal ability, text readability, and reading comprehension. We learn words gradually as we acquire variations in meaning and usage, connections among words, and understanding of that which is unique about words.

Blachowicz, Fisher, Ogle, and Watts-Taffe (1996) remind us that older youths who lack vocabulary exposure meet with frustration when trying to match decoded words to known meanings. Moreover, they have not developed multilayered conceptual associations to allow reading with nuance. By the end of elementary school reading, youths know roughly 25,000 words, a bank that grows to 50,000 words by the end of high school (Graves & Watts-Taffe, 2002). Sadly, older youth who struggle with reading suffer from what Stanovich (1986) called the "Matthew effect" with regard to vocabulary acquisition: those who read less do not develop vocabulary at the same rate as their fluently reading peers.

The National Reading Panel (2000) concluded that vocabulary knowledge is developed implicitly, through wide reading, and explicitly, through instruction that uses multimedia and association methods to teach definitions and other word attributes. Graves and Watts-Taffe (2002) recommend four areas for development: encouraging wide reading, teaching a few carefully selected words, fostering word consciousness, and promoting word-learning strategies. This includes explicit instruction in use of context, common word parts, dictionaries, and other reference tools to unlock the meanings of unknown words (Graves, 2006). Spending precious time explaining thousands of other words already known by other youths seems relatively futile (Richek, 2005).

Developing Strategic Comprehension Knowledge

Underwood and Pearson (2004) pointed out, and NAEP (2005) data confirmed, that too many youths are like those in our clinic who develop fluency and decoding strategies, only to struggle with reading comprehension. Pressley (2002) explained that a host of think-aloud studies gave us ideas of strategies good readers use before, during, and after reading. Strategies used before reading include setting goals, prereading for content and text structure, and activating prior knowledge. Strategies used during reading include rereading to determine importance or to understand difficult ideas, making predictions, inferring such implied ideas as pronoun referents or word meanings, integrating ideas, reflecting on mental images, coming to conclusions, evaluating ideas, and monitoring comprehension problems. After reading, readers reread texts to ensure comprehension, or they recite and reflect on meaning found in texts.

Duke and Pearson (2002) suggested that effective comprehension instruction should address the development of individual strategies and their integration, and include an explicit description of the strategy and when and how it should be used, teacher and/or student modeling of use, collaborative use, guided practice, and independent practice. These authors noted that research supports teaching prediction, think-alouds, use of text structure, visual representation, summarization, and questioning, a list that closely resembles that developed by Pressley (2002) and the National Reading Panel (2000).

Underwood and Pearson (2004) described several levels of comprehension strategies interventions. Level 1 interventions teach learners to create mental representations of text, using text structure and content to differentiate between more and less important ideas, and using graphic organizers to represent text macrostructure. Level 2 interventions teach learners the active behaviors of expert readers, through think-alouds, questioning the author, and question–answer relationships. Level 3 interventions are concerned with helping learners to regulate their own literacy activities within the social world, acknowledging identity and other social constructions, variability across discourse communities, and personal interests in balance with community interests. These authors also envision Level 4 interventions that are concerned with cognitive and social aspects of multiple representation systems and the Internet.

WHAT RESEARCH DOES NOT TELL US ABOUT TEACHING OLDER YOUTHS WHO STRUGGLE WITH READING

Just as high-stakes screening tests cannot give us insight about particular difficulties of youths who struggle with reading, research does not tell us how to facilitate particular youths' literacy development. Research does give us some declarative knowledge of what to do and some procedural knowledge of how to do it. However, research does not provide conditional insights needed to collaborate with older youths on developing interventions to suit their varying profiles.

Our literacy clinic has a history of inviting teachers to implement research-based interventions. This process is not without frustration as teachers realize that research does not tell them specifically what to do, and as our clinicians often offer somewhat competing advice (Hinchman, 1999). What research says about assessment, intervention design, and what to teach becomes quite a bit shakier when we try to determine when to make what pedagogical moves—although youths noting that we teach "what I need to know next" provides some validation for our work (Michel & Dougherty, 1999).

More about Assessment

High-stakes screening tests are not reliable measures of the abilities of those who struggle with reading: such youths often become frustrated and give up when too difficult texts overtax their decoding, vocabulary, or comprehension strategies. These assessments do not allow us to know how successful some individuals could be if testing tasks varied to account for familiarity with passage content, text or sentence structures, or vocabulary. They do not provide enough information for designing an intervention for locating youths who struggle with reading tasks not tested in the screening, such as the reading of longer passages. Repeating the experience within one school year, as is suggested by some schoolwide assessment systems, can be particularly vexing for such youths and their teachers (Sperling, 2006).

In our clinic applications of retrospective miscue analysis and think-alouds, we discovered that collaborating older youths can be willing to talk through any completed literacy task. Walking through a task in a discrete one-to-one setting, respectfully and nonjudgmentally, in response to the query, "Tell me what you were thinking when you did x," can yield valuable diagnostic insights and help youths to develop important self-awareness. Questions into how a youth approaches reading, including figuring out unknown words or drawing inferences, are appropriate. Collaborating young people can collect reading responses and writing in a reflective portfolio so that they can explain them to parents and others as examples of their literacy development (Tierney et al., 1998).

Over time, teachers and youths can have wide-ranging conversations about in- and out-of-school literacy practices. Such conversations depend on rapport between teachers and students. Knowledge of youths' out-of-school activities can inform reading selections, inquiry topics, and strategy instruction. In addition to providing a teacher with important diagnostic information, such interactions develop self-awareness important to youths' literacy proficiency.

More about Intervention Design

Research suggests that older youths' motivation is largely a product of instruction and looms large over intervention attempts (Eccles, Wigfield, & Schiefele, 1998). Current notions of youth identity construction and motivation hint that combining code- and meaning-emphasis interventions could be most valuable for older youths who struggle yet bring out-of-school literacies to the table. Borrowing Luke and Elkins's (2000) notions of re/mediation to connote instruction that invites youths to demonstrate their capabilities, Alvermann (2003) proposed interventions that acknowledge cultural factors affecting students' engagement in reading and follow-up discussions, out-of-school language patterns and cultural practices, realization that content coverage and higher level thinking can be accomplished simultaneously, and use of multiple sources of print and nonprint media. Greenleaf and colleagues (2002) suggested interventions that are developed collaboratively, involving teachers, youths, and parents.

Controversy rages about appropriate research-based instructional responses to older youths who struggle with reading. Some commercial programs for older youths claim to be supported by research from the National Reading Panel (2000) report even though most of the studies in this review were completed with younger children and none gives advice about the design or components of a "best" comprehensive approach (Conley & Hinchman, 2004). Program administrators are frustrated by discussions of curriculum that begin with the words "It depends"—on what youths know and want to know, as well as on what a teacher, a parent, and a youth convince each other are areas of primary need, and, from this, naive decision makers sometimes infer that any program will suffice. However, the actual answer is a more complex, trial-and-error process: once a teacher determines a youth's interests and needs, including an understanding of what the youth thinks "I need to learn next," then the teacher and the youth together can develop an intervention, one that evolves to be increasingly efficient and effective as the relationship grows.

For instance, when a youth struggles with reading fluency and motivation, tutor and youth may negotiate a meaning-based intervention to address motivation, spending the most instructional time completing an Internet inquiry, but practicing fluency strategies as they search. Responsibility for inquiry tasks is gradually and explicitly turned over to the student, with support offered when needed. Tutors will often begin with texts reflecting youths' out-of-school interests, and move into increasingly complex academic texts. A teacher may ask the individual to reread bits of texts aloud or to rehearse a dictated inquiry report to develop fluency (Rasinski & Hoffman, 2003). If fluency difficulties stem from word analysis difficulties, a teacher may use words found during inquiry or used in writing to initiate incidental needed instruction. Intervention for another youth may instead be code-based and focused on word-learning strategies applied to reading.

More about What to Teach

Older youths that we see in our literacy clinic do not usually suffer from a significant lack of phonological awareness or letter–sound knowledge. However, many lack strategies for systematically figuring out unknown words within the context of their reading. Others lack knowledge of how to read multisyllabic words or specific word families, such as vowel teams, which is especially important since the ability to attend to graphophonic cues in the middle of words is thought to be necessary for effective reading (Pressley, Gaskins, Solic, & Collins, 2006).

Vellutino and Scanlon (2002) researched the Interactive Strategies Approach to give emergent readers strategies for answering the question "What do I do when I come to a word I don't know?" This lesson framework spends roughly half the instructional time with a child rereading familiar texts and reading new texts to practice word-level strategies one at a time and then as a collection. The other half of the lesson focuses on the acquisition of such phonological skills as phoneme awareness, letter names, letter sounds, and redundant spelling patterns, as well as on the acquisition of sight vocabulary and writing. Strategies taught and reinforced during reading include checking the pictures, thinking about the sounds in the word, looking for known word families or little words, reading past the puzzling word, going back to the beginning of the sentence and starting again, trying different pronunciations for some of the letters, especially the vowels, and breaking the word into smaller parts.

With the exception of checking the pictures, Vellutino and Scanlon's strategies can be useful for some older readers. Our tutors sometimes ask tutees to rehearse answers to the question "What do I do when I come to a word I don't know?" by printing a discrete strategies checklist onto one side of an index card for referral during reading. They also teach youths to syllabicate, roughly, much as Bhattacharya and Ehri (2004) suggest, by focusing on clustering letters around medial vowels, and explain six useful syllable types (e.g., Blachman, Tangel, Ball, Black, & McGraw, 1999; Moats, 2001; Snow, Griffin, & Burns, 2005), printing them on the other side of the above index card in a list that includes the rule and examples for each (Moore & Hinchman, 2005):

1. Closed syllables, such as *cop* and *hit*, end with vowel–consonant, and the vowel sound is short.
2. Final-*e* syllables, such as *sane* and *Mike*, end with vowel–consonant–silent *e*, with the first vowel long, meaning it says its name.
3. Open syllables, such as the first syllable in *open* and *me*, end with a vowel that is usually a long sound.
4. Vowel team syllables, such as *pain*, *eight*, and *soil*, take the long sound of the first vowel in the team, and, more often, make a new but related sound.
5. Vowel + *r* syllables, such as *bar* and *her*, have the sound of the vowel changed by the *r*, with *ar* and *or* maintaining distinct sounds, while *er*, *ir*, and *ur* make the same sound.

6. Consonant + *le* syllables, such as *purple* and *mottle*, have the consonant *le* syllable making a consonant, short *u*, and /l/ sound.

Older youths we encounter seem to appreciate learning a more systematic approach to reading longer words, often citing "syllable types" as a favorite emphasis of their clinic work, exclaiming, "This is the stuff they haven't been telling me!"

We use Kuhn and Stahl's (2003) teacher-assisted repeated reading in our clinic to help youths develop fluency, usually within the context of preparing for an actual performance. For instance, during the turn taking of interactive guided reading, the teacher talks a bit about how to make reading sound fluent, reads a line or two aloud, and then invites a student to reread and mimic this reading—with an eye toward helping the student seek fluency during all reading. Tutors and students sometimes compose reports, with the student rereading pieces until fluent delivery is achieved. Practice for readers' theater or poetry slams offers other venues for meaningful repeated reading, as well as the opportunity to improve fluency and prosody.

We encourage older youths to increase personal and academic reading, and to attend to and learn newly encountered words—instead of becoming discouraged or giving up from such encounters (Cunningham, 2006). We ask them to see if they can skip such words without losing too much meaning. If not, we suggest they use context clues to make a guess about meaning. Only when a more precise meaning is needed do we recommend available reference tools. Many teachers and students keep vocabulary notebooks and organize word sorts and writing activities around collections of found words. We develop word consciousness by collecting various words found in the youths' world, including the technical vocabulary of out-of-school literacies.

We also encourage tutors to attempt Level 3 or 4 comprehension interventions. Like O'Brien (2003), we may begin with highly scaffolded Internet reading and note taking on topics in which youths are interested, helping them to create multimedia representations. Tutors explain Level 1 text structure, and model such Level 2 active reading strategies as the prediction, questioning, summarizing, and monitoring of Reciprocal Teaching (Palinscar & Brown, 1984). Teachers work their way from personal literacy applications toward organizing inquiries around academic subjects, reading and critiquing primary source documents and Internet sources, and gradually turning over control of strategy selection over time.

Clay (1993) and Fountas and Pinnell (2006) organize both intervention and developmental literacy programs through grade eight by accelerating readers' progress through increasingly more difficult, leveled texts. Despite controversy surrounding text-leveling systems (Cunningham, Spadorcia, & Erickson, 2005), youths in our clinic seem to benefit from similar attention to the readability of texts, especially when they are helped to extend strategy application progressively in increasingly complex material. Similarly, our clinic tutors will often use three books at a time with tutees: one self-selected easy book for independent reading, one instructional-level text for strategy instruction, and one grade-appropriate, more complex text for demonstrating additional text-related problem solving.

RESEARCH WE NEED FOR OLDER YOUTHS WHO STRUGGLE WITH READING

Much research has looked at the construction of valid and reliable measures of reading ability to be used in high-stakes assessments. However, such assessments do not give teachers much in the way of detailed insights about the literacies of the youths with whom they work, and they help to create constructions that blame youths for failing to achieve rather than inappropriate instruction. Johnston (2005) suggested that, instead, the more descriptive a teacher's knowledge of various aspects of students' literacy processes is, the more a teacher is able to design responsive pedagogy. Research we need involves ongoing design of assessments that help us to understand and even celebrate the details of older youths' literacy practices so that we can design pedagogy to advance these practices.

Research we have suggests that interventions to accelerate reading progress should be grounded in youths' interests and goals. Meaning-emphasis intervention can begin at this point, and can be combined with needed development of decoding/encoding, fluency, vocabulary, and comprehension strategies through collaborative apprenticeships with expert readers (Schoenbach, Greenleaf, Cziko, & Hurwitz, 1999). Code-emphasis approaches may be appropriate when youths understand and agree that such approaches give them productive strategies, that is, "teach them what they need to know next," for reading desired texts. Research we need includes that which helps us understand how and when to vary amounts of time spent on such code- or meaning-emphasis negotiated intervention.

Much research suggests that youths shape and are shaped by multiple literacies situated in the various in- and out-of-school spaces within which they find themselves. Indeed, older learners, especially those who struggle with reading, enact such unique mixes of literacy, identity construction, and social group membership that there is a paradox for researchers: what's optimum is more apt to be adapted to an individual's insights and interests than it is to be replicable. Research we need includes that which helps us to understand the strengths of those who struggle with reading and how to foster application and extension of these strengths to additional contexts.

Depending on their strengths and needs, older youths who struggle with reading can benefit from developing strategies to attend to graphosyllabic word features, key vocabulary and word learning, fluency, and comprehension strategies. Yet we have mostly anecdotal ideas of which individuals would most benefit from certain kinds of instruction and why. Given the limited nature of intervention research with older youths to date, there could well be a host of other interventions that help youths bring their strengths to the development of these strategies. Moreover, we have almost no idea of ways to adapt one-to-one interventions for use with less expensive, larger groups. We need research that tells us how to orchestrate larger scale interventions given particular youths' reading profiles—profiles that, as Underwood and Pearson (2004) suggested, attend to cognitive information-processing strategies as well as sociocultural aspects of youth's learning, yielding instruction that teachers and youths agree "teach me what I need to know next."

REFERENCES

Afflerbach, P. (2004). *National Reading Conference policy brief: High stakes testing and reading assessment.* Retrieved February 11, 2007, from *www.nrconline.org*

Allington, R. L. (1994). What's special about special programs for children who find learning to read difficult? *Journal of Reading Behavior, 26,* 95–115.

Allington, R. L. (2002). Research on reading/learning disability interventions. In A. E. Farstrup & S. J. Samuels (Eds.), *What research has to say about reading instruction* (3rd ed., pp. 261–290). Newark, DE: International Reading Association.

Allington, R. L., & Walmsley, S. (1995). *No quick fix: Rethinking literacy programs in America's elementary schools.* New York: Teachers College Press.

Alvermann, D. E. (2001). Reading adolescents' reading identities: Looking back to see ahead. *Journal of Adolescent and Adult Literacy, 44,* 676–690.

Alvermann, D. E. (2003). *Seeing themselves as capable and engaged readers: Adolescents and re/mediated instruction.* Naperville, IL: Learning Point Associates/North

Central Regional Educational Laboratory. Retrieved January 30, 2007, from *www.ncrel.org*

Bear, D., Invernizzi, M., Templeton, S. R., & Johnston, F. (2003). *Words their way* (3rd ed.). New York: Prentice-Hall.

Betts, E. A. (1950). *Foundations of reading instruction, with emphasis on differentiated guidance.* New York: American Book Company.

Bhattacharya, A., & Ehri, L. (2004). Graphosyllabic analysis helps adolescent struggling readers read and spell words. *Journal of Learning Disabilities, 37,* 331–348.

Biancarosa, G., & Snow, C. (2004). *Reading next: A vision for action and research in middle and high school literacy.* Washington, DC: Alliance for Excellent Education.

Blachman, B., Tangel, D., Ball, E. W., Black, R., & McGraw, C. K. (1999). Developing phonological awareness and word recognition skills: A two-year intervention with low-income, inner-city children. *Reading and Writing: An Interdisciplinary Journal, 11,* 239–273.

Blachowicz, C., Fisher, P., Ogle, D., & Watts-Taffe, S. (2006). Vocabulary: Questions from the classroom. *Reading Research Quarterly, 41,* 524–539.

Blackburn, M. (2003). Exploring literacy performances and power dynamics at The Loft: Queer youth reading the world and the word. *Research in the Teaching of English, 37,* 467–490.

Brasseur, I., Gilroy, P., & Schumaker, J. (2004). Profiling the quality of educational programs for adolescents with disabilities. *Teaching Exceptional Children, 37,* 62–65.

Buly, M. R., & Valencia, S. W. (2002). Below the bar: Profiles of students who fail state reading assessments. *Educational Evaluation and Policy Analysis, 24,* 219–239.

Chandler-Olcott, K., & Mahar, D. (2003). "Tech-savviness" meets multiliteracies: Exploring adolescent girls' technology-mediated literacy practices. *Reading Research Quarterly, 38,* 356–385.

Cheatham, J., Colvin, R., & Laminack, L. (1993). *Tutor: A collaborative approach to literacy instruction.* Syracuse, NY: Literacy Volunteers of America.

Clay, M. (1993). *Reading recovery: A guidebook for teachers in training.* Portsmouth, NH: Heinemann.

Conley, M., & Hinchman, K. A. (2004). No Child Left Behind: What it means for America's adolescents and what we can do about it. *Journal of Adolescent and Adult Literacy, 48,* 42–50.

Cunningham, J. W., Spadorcia, S. A., & Erickson, K. A. (2005). Investigating the instructional supportiveness of leveled texts. *Reading Research Quarterly, 40,* 410–427.

Cunningham, P. (2006). What if they can say the words but don't know what they mean? *Reading Teacher, 59,* 708–711.

Diamond, J. B., Corrin, W. J., & Levinson, J. (2004). *Challenging the achievement gap in a suburban high school: A multimethod analysis of an adolescent literacy initiative.* Naperville, IL: Learning Point Associates. Retrieved January 30, 2007, from *www.ncrel.org*

Duke, N. K., & Pearson, P. D. (2002). Effective practices for developing reading comprehension. In A. E. Farstrup & S. Samuels (Eds.), *What research has to say about reading instruction* (pp. 205–242). Newark, DE: International Reading Association.

Eccles, J. S., Wigfield, A., & Schiefele, U. (1998). Motivation to succeed. In W. Damon (Series Ed.) & N. Eisenberg (Vol. Ed.), *Handbook of child psychology* (5th ed., pp. 1017–1095). New York: Wiley.

Ekwall, E., & Shanker, J. (1999). *Ekwall/Shanker reading inventory* (4th ed.). New York: Allyn & Bacon.

Finders, M. (1997). *Just girls: Hidden literacies and life in junior high.* New York: Teachers College Press.

Fountas, I., & Pinnell, G. (2006). *Teaching comprehension and fluency: Thinking, talking, and writing about reading, K–8.* Portsmouth, NH: Heinemann.

Gaskins, R. W., Gaskins, I. W., & Anderson, R. C. (1995). The reciprocal relationship between research and development: An example involving a decoding strand for poor readers. *Journal of Reading Behavior, 27,* 337–377.

Gee, J. P. (1996). *Social linguistics and literacies: Ideology in discourse.* New York: Taylor & Francis.

Gee, J. P. (2006). Self-fashioning and shape-shifting: Language, identity, and social class. In D. E. Alvermann, K. A. Hinchman, D. W. Moore, S. F. Phelps, & D. Waff (Eds.), *Reconceptualizing the literacies in adolescents' lives* (pp. 165–186). New York: Erlbaum.

Good, R., & Kaminski, R. (1996). Assessment of instructional decisions: Toward a proactive/prevention model of decision-making for early literacy skills. *School Psychology Quarterly, 11,* 326–336.

Goodman, Y. M., & Marek, A. M. (1996). *Retrospective miscue analysis.* Katonah, NY: Owen.

Goodman, Y. M., Watson, D. J., & Burke, C. L. (1987). *Reading miscue inventory: Alternative procedures.* New York: Owen.

Graves, M. F. (2006). *The vocabulary book: Learning and strategies.* New York: Teachers College Press (with the International Reading Association and the National Council of Teachers of English).

Graves, M. F., & Watts-Taffe, S. M. (2002). The place of word consciousness in a research-based vocabulary program. In A. E. Farstrup & S. Samuels (Eds.), *What research has to say about reading instruction* (pp. 140–165). Newark, DE: International Reading Association.

Greenleaf, C., Jiménez, R., & Roller, C. (2002). Reclaiming secondary reading interventions: From limited to rich conceptions, from narrow to broad conversations. *Reading Research Quarterly, 37,* 484–496.

Hinchman, K. A. (1999). Querying reflective pedagogy in reading specialists' tutorial practica. In D. H. Evensen & P. B. Mosenthal (Eds.), *Reconsidering the role of the reading clinic in a new age of literacy* (pp. 133–148). Stamford, CT: JAI Press.

Hinchman, K. A., & Zalewski, P. (2001). "She puts all these words in": Language learning for two students in tenth grade social studies. In E. B. Moje & D. O'Brien (Eds.), *Constructions of literacy: Studies of teaching and learning in and out of secondary schools* (pp. 171–192). New York: Erlbaum.

Hull, G., & Schultz, K. (2001). *School's out: Bridging out-of-school literacies with class-room practice*. New York: Teachers College Press.

Hynds, S. (1997). *On the brink: negotiating life and literacy with adolescents*. New York: Teachers College Press.

Iversen, S., & Tunmer, W. (1993). Phonological processing skills and the Reading Recovery program. *Journal of Educational Psychology, 85*, 112–126.

Jiménez, R. (1997). The strategic reading abilities and potential of five low-literacy Latina/o readers in middle school. *Reading Research Quarterly, 32*, 224–243.

Johnson, M. M., & Kress, R. (1965). *Informal reading inventories*. Newark, DE: International Reading Association.

Johnston, P. (2005). Literacy assessment and the future. *Reading Teacher, 58*, 684–686.

Johnston, P., & Allington, R. L. (1991). Remediation. In R. Barr, P. Mosenthal, M. Kamil, & P. D. Pearson (Eds.), *Handbook of reading research* (pp. 984–1012). New York: Longman.

Jones, P., Carr, J., & Ataya, R. (Eds.). (2006). *Pig don't get fatter the more you weigh it.* New York: Teachers College Press.

Knobel, M. (2002). *Everyday literacies: Students, discourse, and social practice*. New York: Lang.

Kuhn, M., & Stahl, S. (2003). Fluency: A review of developmental and remedial practices. *Journal of Educational Psychology, 95*, 13–21.

Laubach, F., Kirk, E. M., & Laubach, R. (1981). *Laubach way to reading*. Syracuse, NY: New Readers Press.

Leander, K. M. (2001). "This is our freedom bus going home right now": Producing and hybridizing space–time contexts in pedagogical discourse. *Journal of Literacy Research, 33*, 637–679.

Leander, K. M. (2002). Locating Latanya: The situated production of identity artifacts in classroom interaction. *Research in the Teaching of English, 37*, 198–250.

Leander, K. M., & Lovvorn, J. F. (2006). Literacy networks: Following the circulation of texts, bodies, and objects in the schooling and online gaming of one youth. *Cognition and Instruction, 24*, 291–340.

Lemke, J. (1990). *Talking science: Language, learning, and values*. Norwood, NJ: Ablex.

Lesko, N. (2001). *Act your age: A cultural construction of adolescence*. New York: Routledge Falmer.

Leslie, L., & Caldwell, J. (2005). *Qualitative reading inventory* (4th ed.). New York: Allyn & Bacon.

Lewis, C., & Fabos, B. (2005). Instant messaging, literacies, and social identities. *Reading Research Quarterly, 40*, 470–501.

Luke, A., & Elkins, J. (2000). Re/mediating adolescent literacies. *Journal of Adolescent and Adult Literacy, 43*, 396–398.

Marzano, R., Pickering, D., & McTighe, J. (1993). *Assessing student outcomes: Performance assessment using the dimensions of learning*. Alexandria, VA: Association of Curriculum and Staff Development.

Michel, P., & Dougherty, C. (1999). Reading clinic: Past, present, and future. In D. H. Evensen & P. B. Mosenthal (Eds.), *Reconsidering the role of the reading clinic in a new age of literacy* (pp. 365–384). Stamford, CT: JAI Press.

Moats, L. (2001). When older students can't read. *Educational Leadership, 58*, 36–40.

Moje, E. B. (2000). To be part of the story: The literacy practices of gangsta adolescents. *Teachers College Record, 102*, 651–690.

Moje, E. B., Ciechanowski, K. M., Kramer, K., Ellis, L., Carrillo, R., & Collazo, T. (2004). Working toward third space in content area literacy: An examination of everyday funds of knowledge and discourse. *Reading Research Quarterly, 39*, 38–70.

Moore, D. W., & Hinchman, K. A. (2005). *Teaching adolescents who struggle with reading: Practical strategies.* New York: Allyn & Bacon.

Moore, D. W., Readence, J. E., & Rickelman, R. J. (1983). An historical exploration of content reading instruction. *Reading Research Quarterly, 18*, 419–438.

National Center for Educational Statistics. (2006). *National assessment of educational progress: The nation's report card: Reading 2005.* Washington, DC: U.S. Department of Education, Institute of Education Sciences. Retrieved January 30, 2007, from *ces.ed.gov/nationsreportcard*

National Center for Educational Statistics. (2007). *National assessment of educational progress: 12th-grade reading and mathematics 2005.* Washington, DC: U.S. Department of Education, Institute of Education Sciences. Retrieved March 15, 2007, from *ces.ed.gov/nationsreportcard*

National Reading Panel. (2000). *Report of the National Reading Panel: Teaching children to read. Report of the subgroups.* Washington, DC: U.S. Department of Health and Human Services, National Institutes of Health.

New London Group. (1996). A pedagogy of multiliteracies: Designing social futures. *Harvard Educational Review, 66*, 60–92.

O'Brien, D. (2003). Juxtaposing traditional and intermedial literacies to redefine the competence of struggling adolescents. *Reading Online, 6*(7). Retrieved February 1, 2007, from *www.readingonline.org/newliteracies/lit_index.asp?HREF=obrien2/*

Palinscar, A. M., & Brown, A. (1984). Reciprocal teaching of comprehension-fostering and comprehension-monitoring activities. *Cognition and Instruction, 1*, 117–175.

Paris, S. G., & Carpenter, R. D. (2003). FAQs about IRIs. *Reading Teacher, 56*, 578–580.

Paris, S. G., Lipson, M. Y., & Wixson, K. K. (1983). Becoming a strategic reader. *Contemporary Educational Psychology, 8*, 293–316.

Pearson, P. D., & Gallagher, M. (1983). The instruction of reading comprehension. *Contemporary Educational Psychology, 8*, 317–344.

Pressley, M. (2002). Metacognition and self-regulated comprehension. In A. E. Farstrup, & S. Samuels (Eds.), *What research has to say about reading instruction* (pp. 291–309). Newark, DE: International Reading Association.

Pressley, M. (2006). *Reading instruction that works: The case for balanced teaching* (3rd ed.). New York: Guilford Press.

Pressley, M., Gaskins, I. W., Solic, K., & Collins, S. (2006). A portrait of Benchmark School: How a school produces high achievement in students who previously failed. *Journal of Educational Psychology, 98*, 282–306.

Pressley, M., Hilden, K., & Shanklin, R. (2006). *An evaluation of end-grade-3 Dynamic Indicators of Basic Literacy Skills (DIBELS): Speed reading without comprehension, predicting little.* Unpublished manuscript, Michigan State University Literacy Achievement Research Center, East Lansing, MI. Retrieved January 30, 2007, from *www.msularc.org/dibels%*

Quatroche, D., Bean, R., & Hamilton, R. (2001). The role of the reading specialist: A review of research. *Reading Teacher, 55,* 282–294.

Rasinski, T., & Hoffman, J. (2003). Oral reading in the school literacy curriculum. *Reading Research Quarterly, 38,* 510–522.

Rasinski, T., & Padak, N. (2006). Fluency beyond the primary grades: Helping adolescent struggling readers. *Voices from the Middle, 13,* 34–41.

Richek, M. (2005). Words are wonderful: Interactive, time-efficient ways to teach meaning vocabulary. *Reading Teacher, 58,* 414–423.

Samuels, S. J. (1979). The method of repeated readings. *Reading Teacher, 32,* 403–408.

Schoenbach, R., Greenleaf, C., Cziko, C., & Hurwitz, L. (1999). *Reading for understanding.* San Francisco: Jossey-Bass.

Shefelbine, J. (1990). A syllabic-unit approach to teaching decoding of polysyllabic words to fourth- and sixth-grade disabled readers. In J. Zutell & S. McCormick (Eds.), *Literacy theory and research: Analysis from multiple paradigms* (pp. 223–230). Chicago: National Reading Conference.

Shefelbine, J., & Calhoun, J. (1991). Variability in approaches to identifying polysyllabic words: A descriptive study of sixth graders with highly, moderately, and poorly developed syllabication strategies. In J. Zutell & S. McCormick (Eds.), *Learner factors/teacher factors: Issues in literacy research and instruction* (pp. 169–177). Chicago: National Reading Conference.

Shefelbine, J., Lipscomb, L., & Hern, A. (1989). Variables associated with second, fourth, and sixth grade students' ability to identify polysyllabic words. In S. McCormick & J. Zutell (Eds.), *Cognitive and social perspectives for literacy research and instruction* (pp. 145–149). Chicago: National Reading Conference.

Snow, C., Burns, M., & Griffin, P. (1998). *Preventing reading difficulties in young children.* Washington, DC: National Academy Press.

Snow, C., Griffin, P., & Burns, M. S. (2005). *Knowledge to support the teaching of reading: Preparing teachers for a changing world.* San Francisco: Jossey-Bass.

Sperling, R. (2006). Assessing reading materials for students who are learning disabled. *Intervention in School and Clinic, 41,* 138–143.

Stanovich, K. (1986). Matthew effects in reading: Some consequences of individual differences in the acquisition of literacy. *Reading Research Quarterly, 21,* 360–407.

Street, B. V. (1995). *Social literacies: Critical approaches to literacy in development, ethnography, and education.* New York: Longman.

Thurlow, M., & Wiley, H. (2006). A baseline perspective on disability subgroup reporting. *Journal of Special Education, 39,* 246–254.

Tierney, R., Clark, C., Fenner, L., Herter, R., Simpson, C., & Wiser, B. (1998). Portfolios: Assumptions, tensions, and possibilities. *Reading Research Quarterly, 33,* 474–486.

Torgesen, J. K., Wagner, R. K., & Rashotte, C. A. (1999). Preventing reading failure in young children with phonological processing disabilities: Group and individual responses to instruction. *Journal of Educational Psychology, 91,* 575–594.

Underwood, T., & Pearson, P. D. (2004). Teaching struggling adolescent readers to comprehend what they read. In T. L. Jetton & J. A. Dole (Eds.), *Adolescent literacy research and practice* (pp. 135–161). New York: Guilford Press.

Van Someren, M. W., Barnard, Y. F., & Sandberg, J. A. C. (1994). *The think-aloud method: A practical guide to modeling cognitive processes*. London: Academic Press.

Vellutino, F., & Scanlon, D. (2002). The Interactive Strategies Approach to reading intervention. *Contemporary Educational Psychology, 27,* 573–635.

Wilson, J. L. (2005). Interrupting the failure cycle: Revaluing two seventh-grade struggling readers. *Voices from the Middle, 12,* 25–31.

3

The Literacy Development of African American Male Adolescents

The Influence of Contexts and Texts

ALFRED W. TATUM

Throughout history, the powers of single black men flash
here and there like falling stars, and die sometimes before
the world has rightly gauged their brightness. . . . Their
youth shrunk into tasteless sycophancy, or into silent
hatred of the pale world about them . . . or wasted itself in
a bitter cry, Why did God make me an outcast and a
stranger in mine own house?
                              —W. E. B. DU BOIS (1901)

Black males are reminded everyday of their poor literacy
ability—"an unrelieved constancy."
                              —LIEBOW (1967)

The "black male reading problem" is presenting a major dilemma for teachers, parents, communities, and the young men themselves. Although the exact percentage is not clear, African American adolescent males from poor communities continue to perform poorly in
reading as assessed by standardized measures. An analysis of National
Assessment of Educational Progress long-term trend reading assessments reveals that only one in 100 African American 17-year-olds can
read and gain information from specialized text. An example of special-

ized text is a science section in a local newspaper (Haycock & Huang, 2001). Many educators feel discouraged by the prospects of moving a large percentage of African American males from basic levels of reading achievement to proficient and advanced levels of reading achievement.

Researchers have yet to clearly define who these young men are. African American adolescent males have been referred to as "urban adolescents," "economically vulnerable students," "at-risk, ethnic minority students," "disadvantaged students," "endangered species," "a problem," and "unsalvageable children" (Ferguson, 2000; Gibbs, 1988; Goodenow & Grady, 1993; Jordan & Cooper, 2003; Spencer, Cunningham, & Swanson, 1995; Stevenson, Davis, Carter, & Elliott, 2003). It is also unclear why reading problems for these young men persists in U.S. schools despite more than 25 years of reading research.

Research involving African American males and their literacy development is in need of expansion. The African American male presence in reading research is dismal, particularly reading intervention experiments published in prominent, peer-reviewed education research journals (Lindo, 2006). Up to this point, the research involving African American males has been limited; has focused on factors that characterize these young men as at risk; has ignored their racialized and gendered identities; and has focused on comparing their academic outcomes in relation to other students (Davis, 2001; Gilbert & Gilbert, 1998; Price, 2000). Also, theoretical and empirical research concerning African American males focuses on pathology and ignores their coping mechanisms (Swanson, Cunningham, & Spencer, 2003).

However, a productive shift in research is occurring that should benefit the literacy development of African American adolescent males. Researchers have begun to look at cultural–ecological variables; to examine how social processes of race, class, and gender are interwoven in literacy; and to analyze the relationship between masculinity and schooling (Gilbert & Gilbert, 1998; Greene & Abt-Perkins, 2003; Lesko, 2000; Swanson et al., 2003; Young, 2000). Gilbert and Gilbert (1998) noted that "addressing the literacy needs of boys have not gone far enough because they have not taken sufficient account of the gendered construction of boys" (p. 200). They added:

> While schools have developed a range of practices that offer help to the "reluctant reader" or the "remedial reader"—both whom are often male—these strategies have not often attempted to engage with the experiences of masculinity such readers bring with them, or critically to

reflect on the ways in which various technologies of literacy learning
might conflict with social constructions of masculinity. (p. 200)

Taking a cultural–ecological stance, Swanson and colleagues (2003)
found that "understanding adolescents from a perspective that considers the interactive nature of culture, context, and gender is particularly
important when research efforts are focused on African American adolescent males" (p. 619). This chapter is informed by this productive
shift in research.

In this chapter, I describe the extant research that provides direction for advancing the literacy development of African American adolescent males while honoring their identities. Second, I identify several
areas of research that are warranted. This chapter focuses on two key
questions:

1. How do in-school and out-of-school contexts impact the literacy development of African American adolescent males from
   poor communities?
2. What implications do in-school and out-of-school contexts have
   for selecting texts to improve the reading achievement of African American adolescent males from poor communities and
   honoring their identities.

I specifically focus on the influences of contexts on the identity construction of African American adolescent males and how texts can be
conceptualized to counter contextual influences that contribute to their
being vulnerable. The chapter ends with implications for research
needed to contribute to the literacy development of African American
adolescent males.

WHY FOCUS ON AFRICAN AMERICAN ADOLESCENT MALES?

One of the primary critiques emerging from the National Reading Panel
Report (2000) commissioned by the U.S. Congress was that there is still
little knowledge about what types of instruction are suitable for different ages and populations of children. This is particularly true for
African American adolescent males from poor communities. Literacy
researchers have given little attention to these young men. The lack of
research became more evident as I searched PsyhInfo and ERIC databases for empirical studies that focused on teaching reading to African

American adolescent males published over the past 30 years. The descriptors "boys," "reading," "adolescent," and "African American" were used in different combinations during the search. For example, the ERIC search yielded 693 results when the descriptors "boys" and "reading" were combined. The combination of "boys," "reading," and "adolescent" yielded 50 results. The combination of "boys," "reading," "adolescent," and "African American/black" yielded no results. The lack of research is problematic for several reasons:

1. Many educators are failing to increase African American male adolescents' engagement with text, and subsequently their reading achievement.
2. Although curriculum is often a significant consideration for improving the educational outcomes for African American males, specific texts and text characteristics that should inform curriculum selection are strikingly absent (Tatum, 2006).
3. There is an absence of research that informs educators how to use texts to counter in-school and out-of-school context-related issues that heighten the vulnerability level of African American males. "Vulnerability level" is defined as the net balance between risk contributors (e.g., poverty, sociocultural expectations, racial stereotypes) and protective factors (e.g., temperament, mental health) (Swanson et al., 2003).

In the next sections, I describe the methodology for this review and its theoretical framing.

REVIEW OF LITERATURE

A multidisciplinary approach was adopted to identify the extant research. The review for this chapter draws upon the work of cultural anthropologists, critical race theorists, educational psychologists, sociologists, and reading researchers who use historical, psychological, and sociological concepts, definitions, frameworks, models, terms, and theories in their research. Quantitative and qualitative reports published in peer-reviewed English journals along with books and edited volumes published in the United States and Australia were identified. In order to qualify for the review, the literature had to be published within the past 20 years and to focus specifically on African American adolescent males.

THEORETICAL FRAMEWORK

This chapter is grounded in a phenomenological variant of ecological systems theory (PVEST) that is relevant for conceptualizing communities and its members from conception to the end of the life course (Swanson et al., 2003). According to Swanson and colleagues (2003), the

> PVEST framework contributes an identity-focused cultural ecological perspective (ICE) on identity formation . . . that takes into account structural and contextual barriers to identity formation and the implication for psychosocial processes such as self-appraisal and enhances our ability to interpret available work and to recommend future improvements on how we structure studies and ask questions about 21st-century experiences of African American males. (p. 612)

This perspective was useful for conceptualizing a chapter that focuses on texts and in-school and out-of-school contexts and how they impact the reading achievement and identity development of African American adolescent males.

OUT-OF-SCHOOL CONTEXTS

The field of adolescent literacy is now giving more attention to students' out-of-school contexts and the molding of adolescents' identities in schools (Davidson, 1996; Hull & Schultz, 2002; Rymes, 2001). Nevertheless, "professionals and researchers often remain clueless about the social and cultural contexts of black males . . . and about how to translate these contexts and experiences into intervention" (Stevenson, 2004, p. 72). Knowledge about these students' family life is often superficial and viewed through distorted cultural representations (Ferguson, 2000). This creates a conceptual gap and limited understanding of how the identities of these young men are shaped in out-of-school environments. This lack of understanding contributes to misinformed pedagogy disconnected from these young men's out-of-school realities.

An increased understanding about the out-of-school contexts of African American adolescent males provides educators with a better pathway for supporting African American adolescent males' negotiation of their identities. These young men have to negotiate among a range of expected roles within their community contexts as they interact with their families, peers, law enforcement, store owners, and other members of their communities. According to Murtadha-Watts (2000), "Negotiation refers to the idea that individual or personal masculine constructions hinge on choice and constraints of various social contexts" (p. 67). There are more constraints in communities with a negative social context.

A community with a negative social context is one that has a high level of poverty (more than 50% of the residents living below the poverty line according to national indices), high levels of residential segregation, limited licit social organization, high levels of unemployment or underemployment, high crime rates, and low-performing elementary, middle, and high schools. A focus is being placed on communities with a negative social context because this is where the lowest performing students usually attend schools. In such communities, African American males are more sensitive to rejection, have greater anxiety for rejection, and react more angrily toward rejection than students who are not similarly situated (Stevenson, 2004). Daily interactions and negotiations within these communities impact their views of literacy.

In a study on the influence of neighborhood quality on adolescents' education values and school support involving 262 single African American mothers and their seventh- and eighth-grade children, researchers found that neighborhood conditions influence early adolescents' beliefs and attitudes about their education, and impoverished neighborhood conditions have a negative impact on school-related outcomes (Ceballo, McLoyd, & Toyokawa, 2004). In another study, African American males were found to be the most vulnerable to neighborhood conditions as evidenced by drop-out rates (Crane, 1991).

However, African American males living in poor neighborhoods have individual and contextual assets that may be used to promote positive behavior and development and could be capitalized on by strength-building interventions (Taylor et al., 2004). Taylor and colleagues (2004) identified internal and external developmental assets that can lead to healthy development. Among them were support, empowerment, social competencies, boundaries and expectations, and positive values. In-school contexts can function as a barrier or conduit to the healthy development of African American adolescent males and the value they place on literacy.

IN-SCHOOL CONTEXT

In schools, low educational achievement functions as a psychosocial stressor and negative feedback increases stress for African American adolescent males (Swanson et al., 2003). African American males' engagement in school is influenced by feelings of psychological membership. Students who have a sense of attachment to the school develop a sense of belongingness that promotes commitment to school goals and to their own engagement and participation in school life (Goodenow, 1993). Goodenow (1993) found that psychological membership is influenced by both personal traits and situational and contextual factors: "Until students resolve where they stand in a particular social setting they [have] difficulty attending to the official tasks at hand" (p. 88). The arbitrary nature of punishments, failure to perceive schools as a personally supportive community, and disdain for the content of the curriculum contributes to school disengagement for African American adolescent males (Price, 2000). Gradual disengagement is the precursor to dropping out of high school for many of these young men (Murtadha-Watts, 2000).

African American males, however, become resilient in school environments that are psychologically hostile when they encounter day-to-day relationships that sustain their commitment to schooling. Price (2000) found that connections seemed important to these young men's sense of self, and a connected relationship for these young men was a person they could trust and share their thoughts and feelings with. In his case study of two African American high school males, he found that the young men were "struggling to define themselves in schooling contexts that were overwhelmingly shaped by institutional and social practices that seemed to perpetuate racial division through privileging some images, representations, and social practices, and subordinating others" (p. 147). Price concluded:

> More attention needs to be given to classrooms, particularly in relation to official curriculum and pedagogy, through promoting discussions with students about the multiple representations of masculinities; . . . about issues of power in relation to class, race, gender . . . ; and about the process of constructing social identities. (p. 157)

Other researchers have found that African American males desire personal connections with their teachers; their identity and appraisal of self and others becomes key, and their awareness of how other perceive them heightens during middle and late adolescence (Davis, 2001; Ferguson, 2000). Based on their perceptions, African American males begin to engage in producing and reproducing what they consider an authentic black masculine identity (Davis, 2001). This reproducing is based on racialized and gender constructions often characterized by a macho identity stance that reflects a striving for identity (Stevenson et al., 2003). This stance, when influenced or informed by negative images of African American maleness, leads to hypervulnerability. *Hypervulnerability* is a heightened sense of gender and racial identity. This stance can ferment into social and personal vulnerabilities as these young men struggle for an African American identity or as they begin to use black masculinity as a tool for coping with negative in-school and out-of-school contexts. Both in-school and out-of-school contexts and their effects on African American adolescent males have real implications for literacy instruction, particularly the role of texts in countering negative contextual forces.

THE TEXT NEGLECT

Research on African American males has given attention to their (1) disengagement, alienation, and poor academic performance in school-related tasks; (2) perceptions and expectations of African American males held by their teachers and how this impacts achievement; (3) racial and gender interactions between students and teachers; (4) environmental and cultural factors that serve as risk variables; (5) relationships among remediation, grade retention, suspensions, and achievement; (6) special education and gifted educational placements; (7) the impact of administrative structures and school policies on the educational performance of African American males; and (8) effective teachers of African American males (Fashola, 2005: Polite & Davis, 1999).

The academic performance of African American males has been examined from multiple perspectives. Psychologists have examined internal factors (e.g., self-concept, identity) that serve as barriers to achievement. Sociologists and anthropologists have looked at societal factors that serve as barriers (e.g., structural racism, community patterns, educational attainment of patterns, socioeconomic status). Educators and literacy theorists have examined in-school factors such as classroom interactions, curricula, and instructional practices. The existing data and research converge on several points:

1. The plight of African American males and the racial achievement gap has unique characteristics.
2. Lack of academic achievement for African American males presents a major crisis.

3. Negative stereotypes, scarcity of positive role models, lack of culturally competent instruction and direction, and problems associated with low socioeconomic status and high-risk neighborhoods are multiple sources of stress and dissonance that characterize the experiences of African American adolescents as they begin the process of self-definition (Swanson et al., 2003).

Several solutions have been offered over the past 10 years to address the literacy needs of African American adolescent males. Among them are (1) providing culturally responsive literacy instruction that links classroom content to students' experiences; (2) developing academically oriented remedial programs, character development programs, rites of passage programs, or comprehensive literacy programs; and (3) establishing all-male academies or alternative schools and programs designed specifically for African American males. In each case it has been offered that African American males need the infusion of African and African American history and culture within a multicultural curriculum. Although we now know more about educating African American males, educators continue to use an anatomically incomplete model to improve their reading achievement by placing most attention on skill and strategy instruction in a nonmeaningful context (Tatum, 2003, 2005). (See Figure 3.1.)

Too often the focus in teaching reading to African American male adolescents suffers from oversimplification and underestimation. This is reflected in the body of Figure 3.1 and highlights the reality that educators and policymakers have focused on skill and strategy instruction while ignoring curriculum orientations, forms of pedagogy, and other factors found to be effective in increasing the reading achievement of students of color. A strong conceptual framework grounded in research related to students' in-school and out-of-school contexts is often neglected.

An anatomically incomplete model to literacy instruction ignores multiple vital components of literacy instruction. (See Figure 3.2.) The vital components of reading include word knowledge and vocabulary, fluency development, strategy knowledge, and language proficiency. The vital components of reading garner the most attention in literacy reform efforts. With the emphasis on skill and strategy instruction to improve reading achievement, other vital components of literacy instruction are overlooked, namely, vital components of read-

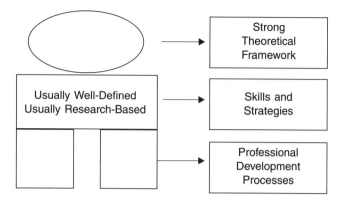

FIGURE 3.1. Anatomically incomplete model of literacy instruction.

ers and educators and vital components of reading instruction. The vital components of readers and educators include home life, culture, environment, language, and economics and their impact on adolescents' literacy development. The vital components of reading instruction encompass the role of quality instructional support, the role of text and contexts, and their combined impact on adolescents' literacy development. In the next section, I bring attention to one of the vital components of reading instruction, text, and its relation to an African American adolescent male striving for identity in negative community contexts.

Reading	Readers and Educators	Educators	Reading instruction
Word knowledge	Home life	Competence	Quality instructional support
Fluency	Culture	Commitment	
Strategy knowledge	Environment	Caring	Text
	Language	Culpability	Context
Language proficiency	Economics		Assessment

FIGURE 3.2. Vital components of literacy instruction.

REBUILDING TEXTUAL LINEAGES

There is a paucity of research that documents information about texts and their relationship to African American males, particularly research that takes into account texts and their relations to larger ideological, political, and economic dynamics (Apple, 1989). Apple (1989) argues that "texts need to be situated in the larger social movements of which they are a part and to ignore text that dominates school curricula as being simply not worthy of serious attention and serious struggle is to live in a world divorced from reality" (p. 104). I have become concerned that the development of textual lineages, that is, texts one finds meaningful and significant to one's development, of African American male adolescents is being severely compromised or severed in an era of accountability. Instead of trying to score with reading with these young men, schools have focused on increasing reading scores. This is problematic because teachers can use text to broker positive, meaningful relationships with African American male adolescents during reading instruction. Powerful texts, in tandem with powerful reading instruction, can have a significant influence on the lives of African American male adolescents despite some of the psychic infections they encounter in negative community contexts. Unfortunately, I am finding that African American male adolescents are suffering from an underexposure to texts that they find meaningful.

Many of these young adolescent males, ranging in age from 11 to 19, are challenged to develop their identities in schools and a society where their identities are continually assaulted. With an increased understanding about in-school and out-school contexts, texts can be selected with a clearer audit of the African American adolescent male. The impact of text on the lives of African American adolescent males cannot be underestimated if the history of text and its influence on African American males are examined. Historically, texts have been central in the literacy development of African American males, with the connections among reading, writing, speaking, and action eminently clear (Tatum, 2005). I then offered that history is laden with enabling texts for African American males. An enabling text is one that moves beyond a sole cognitive focus—such as skill and strategy development—to include a social, cultural, political, spiritual, or economic focus. Unfortunately, African American adolescent males who struggle with reading are encountering texts that are characteristically disabling. A disabling text reinforces a student's perception of being a struggling reader. A disabling text also ignores students' local contexts and their desire as adolescents for self-definition. These disabling texts will not close the reading achievement gap in a race-based and class-based society.

A QUALITATIVE CASE STUDY

In an attempt to identify texts that are enabling, texts moving one to be, do, and act differently as a result of reading and discussing the text, I conducted a qualitative case study with Quincy, a 16-year-old African American adolescent male from one of Chicago's inner-city neighborhoods. He was retained in eighth grade three times. His family lived in a high-crime area where the blue lights of police cameras flashed 24 hours each day. He describes his neighborhood the following way:

"I know the west side of Chicago is ghetto. . . . Like you see all African Americans. I see a lot of them going to school, catching buses, whatever, as good, but in a way you still got that other, you know what I am saying, 35% that is out there on corners or walking the streets, comin' for drugs. There is a lot of that out there, just a lot of dealin' out there, a lot of money laundering and stuff. On my little three block Mona, Mavis, and Monte, where I stay at, there may be a lot of kids but all blocks got drugs on them. . . . It's like a drug house or something. In that three-block area you see cars, everything, police cars comin' through 24-7."

Quincy's biological father, raised in the same neighborhood, was incarcerated. His father's incarceration had a negative effect on Quincy. He shared with me that his dad's going to jail really hurt him and that his grades suffered as a result. Quincy was beginning to travel the same illicit path as his father when we met. He spent some time in a courtroom for a stealing a car. At the same time, he harbored a resilient quality. When I asked him about the impact of the neighborhood on him, he shared: "I'd say it don't really bother me . . . I don't think about it because mostly I'm doing my stuff right." Later in our conversation he added, "I think it is like you make your own predicament. Make sure you're on the right track, make sure I don't make the same type of mistakes." He was referring to mistakes stemming from observing other African American males:

"Wherever you go you see the average black male right on the corner. Wherever you go in the prison you'll see the average black male in prison. Or, you'll see an average black male in a fight, or killing somebody, or they kidnapping for instance, basically doing wrong."

Although Quincy was withstanding some of the negative community contexts, he was struggling to negotiate his identity with his family. "They all think I am dumb," he stated. He was experiencing an out-of-school psychological overload that was affecting his view of himself.

I decided to help Quincy become a better reader in hopes of reshaping his identity so that he would not continue to engage in negative activities. Therefore, I designed a study to identify and describe the aspects of texts that he found most useful for improving his reading and shaping his identity. The primary goal of the study was to gather his views on how reading materials affected the way he viewed himself. Quincy agreed to participate in the study by agreeing to read books, articles, newspaper clippings, and speeches I recommended. He was given the final decision about the materials he chose to read.

Quincy's participation was a major first step because, not only was he a poor reader, but he also suffered from an underexposure to text. He had never read anything that affected him and he had never completed a book. Essentially, he was striving for identity without the benefit of having read texts that could potentially inform his identity development. During our first interview he shared: "To say the truth, I ain't read a book." He then informed me that his teachers did not assign books at school.

It was clear by the end of the first interview that Quincy was experiencing an imbalance between an out-of school literacy overload and an in-school literacy underload (Tatum, 2006). This imbalance often shapes a trajectory of negative life outcomes, particularly for African American adolescent males when in-school literacy instruction fails to help them figure out what they want to do with the rest of their lives. Therefore, I decided to initially select text that would help Quincy critique and understand his experiences on the outside of school. The major criterion was identifying texts that would provide Quincy with capital to become resilient amid some of his negative environmental conditions. *Yo', Little Brother* (Davis & Jackson, 1998) and *Handbook for Boys: A Novel* (Myers, 2002) were among the first texts I recommended.

Countering Dissonance-Producing Contexts

During the second week of the study, Quincy discussed his reading of the text *Yo', Little Brother.* I initiated the conversation by asking Quincy

to discuss how he was affected by the book. He responded, "I just know it helped me out with a lot of problems I had. I wish I had this book earlier so I can know more things about life." During the discussion, Quincy cited 21 subtitles without looking at the table of contents when I asked him to describe and explain parts of the text that stood out to him. I asked him how he remembered so much. He shared: "I mean, cause, I have been through a lot of stuff during the 16 years of my life. It ain't been no bad stuff, but it is some stuff that is good enough to make me remember these titles in these book."

I asked Quincy to describe the impact, if any, the book had on him. The end of our conversation is below:

> TATUM: What do you think you will do differently after reading this book?
>
> QUINCY: I think I should go and take care of myself.
>
> TATUM: Is that what you really think you will do after reading this book?
>
> QUINCY: Yeah, I think I would.
>
> TATUM: But these are just words on the page.
>
> QUINCY: But I understand what [the authors] are saying, where [they are] coming from.

Understanding the authors' message in relations to his lived experiences moved Quincy to rethink his actions in dissonance-producing out-of-school contexts where he was beginning to engage in illicit activities.

Electing Adaptive Solutions

While reading *A Handbook for Boys*, Quincy began to identify parallels between his life and the life of the young man in the novel. When asked to describe what he liked about the text Quincy stated:

> "What I like about this book is a young boy and he had people that stayed on him about his problems. They talked to him. Like in the beginning he went to court for beating up a boy and a judge had him go to a place where a person keep him out of trouble or something."

Quincy began to reflect on his personal experience with the criminal justice system. He shared:

"I just got to learn from the mistakes that [the characters] in the story make, that they telling about in the book. And if I do that, maybe it will make me better before I go out and make the mistakes that they made. I already made a mistake and I am trying to learn from it. I just hope that I don't make any more mistakes. I try to keep my life going and keep my life better."

Very similar to the first book Quincy read, the text drew Quincy into the story and moved him to give the text a chance. He offered:

" . . . It was like I was in the story myself. I was understanding what [the characters] were talking about. It was like I was reading and visualizing what was happening and putting my feet in his shoes."

Quincy gave the texts a chance because they connected to his personal backdrop, his community backdrop, his gender backdrop, and his social backdrop. He used the text to critique his own life. The chapter "Does Life Work?" appealed to Quincy. He stated, "When I read that title I had thought about it for a minute. So, I just got to reading." When I asked him if life works, he responded, "I mean life works but it ain't going to work if you ain't doing right to make your life better." Below is an excerpt from our conversation that illustrates how Quincy began to engage in self-reflective behaviors stimulated by reading the texts.

TATUM: How do you think this text will help you think about your life?

QUINCY: Think about the mistakes I made. Maybe I need to just take my time, calm down, and think about things, think about stuff that I do before I do it and learn from the mistakes. Because you might do a mistake that might mess up your life for real. You might do something to get put in jail and it's going to mess up your life when you come out of jail. . . . This book tell you the truth from the cover. . . . Until I started reading it, what made me really start reading it is because he caught a case and I had a case. I wanted to see what was going to happen in the story. I wanted to see what was going to happen to him. Then maybe, I could learn from his mistake. . . . Since I've been in sixth grade I've been making mistakes. I've been making bad mistakes that's messing me up right now today. From my mistakes right now I am not in school. I supposed to be a junior,

but I'm not there yet. I'm letting all my family pass me up be-
sides my brother, and that's hurting me because now some people look at me as a dummy. . . . The reason I'm trying not to
make mistakes is because every chance I get I make a mistake.

TATUM: Have you ever shared that with anyone?

QUINCY: To tell you the truth, I wouldn't express myself to nobody—
even my grandmother and I love talking to her.

Quincy became extremely reflective because of the text that provided
him with insight into his own existence. The texts moved him to act on
his own life.

Ten weeks into the study and after reading several texts that were
selected to pay attention to his out-of-school psychological scarring,
Quincy began to hold himself accountable for his out-of-school behaviors. After being out of school for several months, he successfully enrolled himself in an alternative high school. This was a major step.
Quincy made the decision to approach the school after his mother re-
fused to enroll him. She was giving up on the young man and becoming
despondent and pessimistic about his ability to succeed.

The texts Quincy were reading functioned as enabling texts that
moved him to act on his own life. I wanted to know if he attributed
changes in his behaviors to the reading materials. He shared: "I'm starting to think. Before I started reading, I didn't think period. So what I am
saying now is I'm starting to think about things. Before I started reading
I didn't really care. I just did what I do." When I asked him if the change
was directly related to reading, he offered:

> "I don't know what it is to tell the truth, but it's got to be reading or
> something. Because before I started reading I stayed in trouble.
> Normally, I don't help my momma clean up, I be cleaning up myself
> for her. The books ain't told me nothing about cleaning up and learn
> how your parents are stressing out. But, like I said I am starting to
> see stress in them. I don't know what it is but I'm changing a little
> bit."

In 10 short weeks that involved the discussion of texts, Quincy actions
began to indicate that texts paying attention to his out-of-school contexts were providing him with a roadmap toward resilience. He was
strengthening his resilience outside of school and hoping to practice
that same resilience once he returned to school.

Experiencing In-School Literacy Underload

During our first meeting following Quincy's reenrollment it became obvious that he was experiencing an in-school literacy underload characterized as low-quality education that did not match the promise of texts we had discussed up until his return. He shared:

> "Since I have been going to school lately it is like the teachers do not care. It's like they just teach things just thrown on grade level just to get out of class. Go to your next class. Make sure you get good grades. Like teaching you stuff you already know. Why don't [they] just go to something new? Sometimes it is just good for us to work hard you know what I am saying, than to work easy. If you give us some easy work we are going to finish in a minute. Give us something we have to sit down and think about."

When I asked Quincy to describe the reading materials, he offered:

> "We ain't been reading nothing. We do work sheets and stuff like all we been doing is working on conflicts and stuff, that's all. And it's like it's got nothing to do with literature."

Ironically, Quincy and I were meeting to discuss two poems, "Does the World Care if I Exist" (Tatum, 2005) and "Life through My Eyes" by Tupac Shakur, a slain African American rapper. Quincy identified the following stanza as meaningful:

> Hell, you can't even teach me how to read—Mr. and Mrs. Teacher
> Then you flunk me, and blame it on me
> Some of it's my fault
> Probably some of my momma's fault as well
> But you're at fault, too
> So, I'll sling a little to get paid
> Get a little respect while I'm at it, maybe get laid

He shared:

> "There was another part I liked. They talking about teachers in school. He was saying like part of it was his fault, his parents fault, and the teacher's fault. That is how he worked his way out of it cause he has got to do the work his self. He just can't depend on nobody else. It is the majority of the teacher's fault because like they teach us

what they supposed to teach. They don't teach anything that is going to help the students. . . . It is just like you get assigned a list of assignments that you want the class to learn but it ain't like what the class needs."

I asked Quincy to explain exactly what he meant. Part of the interview follows:

TATUM: Is that happening in your school now?

QUINCY: So so, but not like all of them. I say one teacher is teaching us stuff that we don't need to learn—that ain't even got to do with what we need to learn either.

TATUM: Give me an example.

QUINCY: For instance, don't laugh. This might be funny, but don't laugh. My teacher, one of my teachers teaching us literature, right, but he doing measurements and stuff. Ain't literature something like reading?

TATUM: Yes, literature is about reading texts.

QUINCY: We don't even have no books. The only thing we got books for is science.

Quincy was experiencing an in-school underload that was unable to compete with the life outcome trajectory being shaped outside of school. He keenly recognizes the dichotomy of meaningful and non-meaningful instruction. At the same time, he embraced that it was his responsibility as reflected in his words, "Cause he has got to do the work his self. He just can't depend on nobody else." However, the lack of text is a major barrier to Quincy's identity negotiation and better reading in this instance. The hope of getting back on track as a result of reading text on the outside of school was diminishing in the alternative high school setting. This was a mismatch between his reenrolling and the absence of text that moved him beyond his out-of-school contexts.

Sadly, Quincy dropped out of the study following his father's release from prison. I lost contact with the young man for more than 2 months. He resurfaced in my life on a Sunday afternoon when I received a telephone call that he was arrested for possessing a small quantity of crack cocaine. Quincy surrendered to the out-of-school overload that destroy the lives of many African American adolescent males, particularly when there is an in-school literacy underload characterized by an underexposure to written texts in a supportive environment that help these young men critique their existence and nurture resilience in negative community contexts.

THE RESEARCH WE NEED

In the chapter, I focused on the role of contexts and texts on the literacy development of African American adolescent males living in communities that contribute to their being vulnerable in school and society. A multidisciplinary approach was taken. Yet it becomes clear from reading this chapter that there are many gaps in the field of literacy research involving African American adolescent males. More carefully controlled studies in schools where we find African American adolescent males who struggle with reading are needed to complement suggested best practices found in descriptive and qualitative studies.

Second, there is a need to include the voices of African American adolescent males in literacy research. While qualitative case study research provides powerful data, there is a need to conduct large-scale research studies that look at the literacy development of African American adolescent males. This can potentially guard against essentializing the African American male adolescent literacy experience in the United States.

Third, more attention needs to be given to text types, characteristics of texts, and the role of texts in advancing the literacy development of African American males. There is ample historical precedent of the role of text in shaping the lives of African American males in the United States. This ample precedent is often overlooked when making curricular decisions to improve the reading outcomes of African American males. I have identified three major research considerations for examining texts and their role in the literacy development of African American males taking out-of-school contexts into consideration. They are (1) texts that function as intermediaries to grant psychosocial membership in schools, (2) texts that counter dissonance-producing contexts, and (3) texts that support identity negotiation.

FINAL WORD

Taking on a life-course perspective (Mizell, 1999) that aligns neatly with cultural–ecological theories that have an analytical bend toward out-of-school and in-school contexts, students' identities, and structural barriers that exists in a highly stratified class-based, race-based society requires a broader conceptualization of texts and their role in shaping the literacy development of African American adolescent males who can be both resilient and vulnerable at the same time. As educators continue to strive to "get it right," many of these young men are surrendering their life chances before they get to know their life choices. In many ways, the lives of African American males continue to be expendable both in schools and out. More literacy research is warranted, particularly research that pays attention to the role of texts in their literacy development. Too many of these young men are suffering from an underexposure to texts in schools—an underexposure that can cause many to go under. This is the lesson we learned from Quincy, who tried to give text a chance, but the texts he received in school missed the mark.

REFERENCES

Apple, M. (1989). *Teachers and texts: A political economy of class and gender in relation in education.* New York: Routledge.

Ceballo, R., McLoyd, V., & Toyokawa, T. (2004). The influence of neighborhood quality on adolescent's educational values and school effort. *Journal of Adolescent Research, 19*(6), 716–739.

Crane, J. (1991). The epidemic theory of ghettos and neighborhood effects on dropping out and teenage childbearing. *American Journal of Sociology, 96,* 1226–1259.

Davidson, A. (1996). *Making and molding identity in schools: Student narratives on race, gender, and academic engagement.* Albany: State University of New York.

Davis, A., & Jackson, J. (1998). *Yo', little brother.* Chicago: African American Images.

Davis, J. (2001). Transgressing the masculine: African American boys and the failure of schools. In W. Martino & B. Meyenn (Eds.), *What about the boys?* (pp. 140–153). Philadelphia: Open University Press.

Du Bois, W. E. B. (2001). *The education of black people: Ten critiques, 1906–1960.* New York: Monthly Review Press.

Fashola, O. (2005). *Educating African American males: Voices from the field.* Thousand Oaks, CA: Corwin Press.

Ferguson, A. (2000). *Bad boys: Public schools in the making of black masculinity.* Ann Arbor: University of Michigan Press.

Gibbs, J. T. (Ed.). (1988). *Young, black, and male in America: An endangered species.* Dover, MA: Auburn House.

Gilbert, R., & Gilbert, P. (1998). *Masculinity goes to school.* New York: Routledge.

Goodenow, C. (1993). The psychological sense of school membership among adolescents: Scale development and educational correlates. *Psychology in the Schools, 30,* 79–91.

Goodenow, C., & Grady, K. (1993). The relationship of school belonging and friends to academic motivation among urban adolescents. *Journal of Experimental Education, 62*(1), 60–71.

Greene, S., & Abt-Perkins, D. (2003). *Making race visible: Literacy research for cultural understanding.* New York: Teachers College Press.

Haycock, K., & Huang, S. (2001). *Are today's high school graduates ready?: Thinking K–16.* Washington, DC: Education Trust.

Hull, G., & Schultz, K. (2002). *School's out!: Bridging out-of-school literacies with classroom practice.* New York: Teachers College Press.

Jordan, W., & Cooper, R. (2003). High school reform and black male students: Limits and possibilities of policy and practice. *Urban Education, 38*(2), 196–216.

Lesko, N. (2000). *Masculinities at school.* Thousand Oaks, CA: Sage.

Liebow, E. (1967). *Tally's Corner: A study of Negro streetcorner men.* Boston: Little, Brown.

Lindo, E. (2006). The African American presence in reading intervention experiments. *Remedial and Special Education, 27*(3), 148–153.

Mizell, C. A. (1999). Life course influences of African American men's depression: Adolescent parental composition, self-concept, and adult earnings. *Journal of Black Studies, 29*(4), 467–490.

Murtadha-Watts, K. (2000). Theorizing urban black masculinity construction in an African-centered school. In N. Lesko (Ed.), *Masculinities at school* (pp. 49–71). Thousand Oaks, CA: Sage.

Myers, W. D. (2002). *Handbook for boys: A novel.* New York: HarperTrophy.

National Reading Panel. (2000). *Teaching children to read: An evidence-based assessment of the scientific research literature on reading and its implications for reading instruction* (NIH Pub. No. 00-4754). Washington, DC: U.S. Department of Health and Human Services.

Polite, V., & Davis, J. (1999). *African American males in school and society: Practices and policies for effective education.* New York: Teachers College Press.

Price, J. (2000). Peer (dis)connections, school, and African American masculinities. In N. Lesko (Ed.), *Masculinities at school* (pp. 127–159). Thousand Oaks, CA: Sage.

Rymes, B. (2001). *Conversational borderlands: Language and identity in an alternative urban high school.* New York: Teachers College Press.

Spencer, M. B., Cunningham, M., & Swanson, D. (1995). Identity as coping: Adolescent African-American males' adaptive responses to high-risk environments. In H. Harris, H. Blue, & E. Griffith (Eds.), *Racial and ethnic identity: Psychological development and creative expression* (pp. 31–52). New York: Routledge.

Stevenson, H. C. (2004). Boys in men's clothing: Racial socialization and neighborhood safety as buffers to hypervulnerability in African American adolescent males. In N. Way & J. Chu (Eds.), *Adolescent boys: Exploring diverse cultures of boyhood* (pp. 59–77). New York: New York Press.

Stevenson, H. C., Davis, G., Carter, R., & Elliott, S. (2003). Why black males need cultural socialization. In H. Stevenson (Ed.), *Playing with anger* (pp. 61–85). Westport, CT: Praeger.

Swanson, D., Cunningham, M., & Spencer, M. B. (2003). Black males' structural conditions, achievement patterns, normative needs, and "opportunities." *Urban Education, 38*(5), 608–633.

Tatum, A. W. (2003). *Advancing the literacies of African American adolescents: A case study of professional development.* Unpublished doctoral dissertation, University of Illinois–Chicago.

Tatum, A. W. (2005). *Teaching reading to black adolescent males: Closing the achievement gap.* Portland, ME: Stenhouse.

Tatum, A. W. (2006). Engaging African American males in reading. *Educational Leadership, 63*(5), 44–49.

Taylor, C., Lerner, R., Eye, A., Bobek, D., Balsano, A., Dowling, E., et al. (2004). Internal and external developmental assets among African American male gang members. *Journal of Adolescent Research, 19*(3), 303–322.

Young, J. P. (2000). Boy talk: Critical literacy and masculinities. *Reading Research Quarterly, 35*(3), 312–337.

4

Responsive Literacy Teaching in Secondary School Content Areas

ELIZABETH BIRR MOJE

This chapter has the daunting task of reviewing the research on responsive literacy teaching in the secondary school content areas and, in effect, of proposing a future research agenda to add flesh to the skeleton of research we already have on responsive literacy teaching at the secondary level. In truth, the body of research is not skeletal, but it may need to be more connected or more organized. To accomplish that task, I have decided to take what might be an unusual stance on responsive literacy teaching by reviewing work on *disciplinary literacy.*

Some might reasonably ask how a phrase that emphasizes the *disciplines* rather than *youth* or *students* or *cultures* could possibly be considered *responsive* teaching. I argue that although the turn among adolescent literacy scholars to focusing on students—a turn in which I participated and tried to advance—was critically important, our field has lost its focus on what responsiveness is supposed to do for students. It is time that we stop for a moment and ask ourselves about our ultimate goal. Is it enough to know our students? Is our goal simply to build relationships with students? Do we want to make them feel good? Or should teachers engage in responsive pedagogy to teach something? That question is obviously facetious, and yet much of the theory and research on the need for responsive pedagogy stop at the gathering of

58

knowledge about students' backgrounds and interests. Theory and research about the *learning goals* of responsive pedagogy has been more elusive, especially at upper levels of secondary schooling, where the content concepts to be learned are often abstract and generally difficult to connect to youths' everyday lives. It seems important that as a field we specify the learning goals of responsive pedagogy within the secondary school disciplines and then map out the requirements for engaging in sophisticated and generative responsive literacy teaching practices in these different subject matter areas.

Equally elusive is a theorization of how to assess whether responsive literacy pedagogy is successful at achieving its goals, regardless of whether the goal is simply to engage students in deep learning or to produce students with deep knowledge or to produce students with strong knowledge production skills (i.e., strong literacy and communication skills). The field lacks the methodologies necessary for documenting multiple forms of growth over time as a result of engagement in responsive literacy teaching and learning activities. The kind of methods to which I refer will, of necessity, be more than standardized tests *and* more than thick descriptions or pattern-based analyses. We need to develop ways to assess the range of skills, strategies, dispositions, and knowledge that youths learn when we respond to who they are and take them to new levels of learning.

In what follows, I explain what I mean by the phrase "responsive pedagogy," and then I review research related to what I consider to be different forms of disciplinary literacy pedagogy, making the argument that these forms, especially if taken together, could be considered the strongest form of responsive pedagogy we could produce.

WHAT IS RESPONSIVE PEDAGOGY?

For a full definition of the construct of *responsive pedagogy*, I refer readers to a chapter I previously coauthored with Kathleen Hinchman (Moje & Hinchman, 2004). In brief, the idea of cultural responsiveness in teaching—or of responsiveness, more generally speaking—is that teachers must not only know the backgrounds and experiences of their students, but also draw from those backgrounds—or "funds of knowledge" (Moll, 1992) to build respectful and rich learning environments for students. Such teaching recognizes that students' needs and interests are mediated by memberships in many different—and sometimes conflicting—groups of people and by activities engaged in many different times, spaces, and relationships (Gee, 1996; Heath, 1983; Lee, 2001; Moll, 1992).

However, it is not enough simply to respond to students' cultural backgrounds and commitments. For responsive literacy pedagogy at the secondary level to achieve its goals, it should not only respond to many different aspects of youths' experience, but draw from and *expand* the possible domains of youths' experience. Moll and Gonzalez (1994) argue, in particular, that the goal of a funds-of-knowledge framework is not simply to celebrate the extensive funds of knowledge in children's lives, but also to use those funds as levers, foundations, and sites for expanding what children already know. Similarly, Carol Lee's (2001) work on cultural modeling is as much about bringing youths into conversation with the discipline of English language and literature as it is about valuing what youths bring to classroom learning. In short, responsive pedagogy in secondary subject matter areas should respond not only to the knowledge, experiences, and practices of youths but also to the knowledge, experiences, and practices of the disciplinary subject matter areas. Moreover, given the focus on literacy and language, responsive literacy pedagogy should account for and respond to the texts and literacy practices of youths and then connect those texts and practices to the texts and literacy practices of the disciplines.

Given these demands for successful responsive literacy pedagogy, it seems that responsive literacy pedagogy requires (1) knowledge of young people, (2) knowledge of the disciplines and/or the secondary school subject areas, and (3) knowledge of texts and literate practices that are valued and privileged in both. In what follows, I review the research we have on each of these points.

THE RESEARCH WE HAVE ON RESPONSIVE
LITERACY TEACHING AT THE SECONDARY LEVEL

What Do We Know about Young People, Their Texts, and Their Literacies?

The question asked in the heading of this section is an interesting one because, in point of fact, we know a great deal about small, localized groups of youths, but much of what is often claimed about young people's literacy skill and practice is based on particular groups whose practices have been generalized to all or on stereotypical representations of youths. For example, many claims are made about adolescent literacy skill levels. Recent years have seen increased press about an alleged adolescent literacy crisis, based on, among other things, data from the National Assessment of Educational Progress (Donahue, Daane, & Grigg, 2003; Perie, Grigg, & Donahue, 2005) and the American College Testing Service (2006). These assessments show declines in achievement among youths as they move from fourth to eighth to 12th grades (although these are not, of course, actually the same students tested at each wave). Generally, however, fourth-grade students' scores are higher than are eighth-grade students' scores and eighth graders' scores are higher than 12th-grade students' scores. In the advanced and proficient categories, 12th-grade scores increase (more students appear to attain proficiency) (Perie et al., 2005), but these unusual increases must be understood in the context of extremely high attrition rates, especially in urban high schools. The data also show cross-sectional declines at 12th grade and flat-to-declining levels of achievement at eighth grade. For example, the percentage of eighth-grade students performing at or above basic literacy levels in 1998 was one point lower than the achievement of eighth graders in 2003 and identical (73%) to the achievement of 2005 eighth graders (Perie et al., 2005).

At first glance, it seems clear from these data that we now have some dismal research about 21st-century adolescents' literacy skills. But is it so clear? It is clear that we should be concerned about these data and that real challenges exist for youths as a consequence of undeveloped literacy skills. However, these data themselves provide us with little information about the causes of the declines we are witnessing. What is behind these failures? Who is involved? And what does it mean, really, to score at different levels on these assessments? Is it the case that youths are reading and writing with less proficiency, or is it the case that they are not willingly participating in testing regimes? Is it the case that youths' reading and writing skills are declining, or is it the case that the demand for higher levels of skills is on the rise, as suggested by popular books such as Friedman's *The World Is Flat* (2005) or by Bill Gates's (2005) popular critique of the uselessness of the skills schools currently teach our nation's youths.

Similarly, popular claims are also often made about how little young people read (which seems amusing in the face of the claim that youths are wired into Internet sites and computer/video games, many of which are littered with print). Nevertheless, the popular claim is that young people do not read, and they certainly do not read books (National Endowment for the Arts, 2004). In this case, however, a number of studies call this claim into question. In terms of reading books, 241 participants in our study responded to a free-response task to describe a favorite book and indicate why it was a favorite, with 77% of survey respondents nominating a favorite book by name. Fiction books accounted for 68% of all nominated books and nonfiction books accounted for 8%. To the question, *Do you consider yourself a writer,* 86% responded, "Yes, I am a writer." Thus, across a range of small- and large-scale studies, there is ample evidence to call into question the claim that adolescents do not read. The questions of what they read, for what reasons, and with what degree of proficiency, though, remain salient.

In terms of why youths read various texts, we have analyzed the following patterns in the explanations Detroit youths gave in both surveys and interviews. First, books needed the reflection of "real life" in relation to space, socioeconomic status, gender, race, or age, but not necessarily all of these at once. In other words, texts do not have to match a reader's identity "perfectly," but rather must feel "real" (see also VanDerPloeg & Moje, 2004). Youths also look for texts with an ability to impart life lessons (e.g., resilience/survival, inspiration). In a similar vein, they seek texts that are useful, offering practical knowledge and solutions to life dilemmas or relational tensions. Many of the young women in our sample—and some of the young men—talk about the importance of books that either model or help them work through relationships with friends, family, and romantic partners (e.g., *Chicken Soup for the Teenage Soul* [Canfield, Hansen, & Kirberger, 1997] is a favorite, as are several books by Carlos Cuauhtemoc Sanchez [e.g., Cuauhtemoc Sanchez, 1995]). Several of the young people with whom we work also suggested that the writing style of books mattered, probably as much for whether they continued to read a text as for whether they were attracted to it in the first place. Because many of them seek out texts for entertainment purposes, urban books (e.g., *The Outsiders* [Hinton, 1967]) and suspense books such as *Flowers in the Attic* (Andrews, 1979) and *Harry Potter and the Prisoner of Azkaban* (Rowling, 1999) are high on their lists.

A number of studies have also argued that young people read and write both to enact and to explore identities and the challenges of their lives (Camitta, 1993; Ciechanowski & Moje, 2002; Finders, 1997; Ingalls, 2005; Lam, 2004; O'Connor, 1996; Shuman & Blue, 1999; Stanley, 2003; VanDerPloeg, 2006). These literate practices are thus powerful ways for young people to engage with the world while they also make decisions about who they want to be and what they want to do.

Although narrative fiction reading is typically lauded as an important way to construct selves and learn to enact identities, many youth literacy and culture scholars have observed young people using a variety of textual media to make sense of who they are and to build and maintain important social relationships (Black, 2006; Chandler-Olcott & Mahar, 2003; Cowan, 2005; Lewis & Fabos, 2005; Gustavson, 2007; Leander & Lovvorn, 2006). Alvermann (2001), for example, demonstrated the extensive reading involved in one young man's Pokemon card habit; Gustavson (2007) examined the role of literacy in a host of out-of-school practices of three young men he studied; Mahiri (2003) and colleagues offer a collected volume filled with studies of the prowess and power of the everyday literacies—print-based and otherwise—of youths. And in my own Detroit-based research, 96% of the 743 youths surveyed reported reading some kind of text three to four times a week or more, with the most commonly cited texts being websites (see cautionary data in previous paragraph), letters and notes on paper, email, music lyrics, novels, and magazines.

One additional claim about youths is the popular perception—generated both by the popular press and by youth literacy researchers—that youths are *wired* (i.e., connected to the Internet, to iPods or MP3 players, or to video and computer games). This perception is largely based in representations of middle- and upper-middle-class youth who have easy and instant access to the hardware and software necessary for such wired states of being. Some research calls into question this claim, however. In just one high-poverty community in Detroit, for example, 51% of the youths report accessing the Internet once a week or less and writing email less than once a month (Moje, Overby, Tysvaer, & Morris, in press). It is also worth noting that within that same sample, the 49% remaining report accessing the Internet and writing email every day. Thus, when an average of the group is taken—or if only one subset of the group had been studied—Internet and email access would have appeared to range from three times a week to daily use. In other words, *who* gets studied and in what numbers matters a great deal to what we know about who young people are as readers and writers.

In sum, what we know about young people may be more about what we think we know—that is, that there are many myths and stereotypes about their skills and their dispositions. What we can say from research is that something is interfering with young people's demonstration of literate skill on national assessments. We also know that what youths read and write both in and out of school are not the texts of their teachers' or policymakers' youth. Furthermore, these texts and young people's purposes for reading them may not promote school achievement as it is traditionally conceived. We are also beginning to understand that young people of different backgrounds, experiences, and economic status have access to different kinds of texts; in general, however, most youths are shaped by some sort of popular culture texts and most appear to both engage in and produce youth cultural texts that are often aligned with popular cultural texts. What those texts look like and how they are engaged and produced may differ radically across groups. Most important, these literate practices appear to have real power in the lives of youths and cannot be ignored.

What Do We Know about the Subject Areas, Their Texts, and Their Literacies?

The simple answer to this question is "Not enough." Lee and Spratley (2007) have begun a project to map the different practices of different disciplines, but the work is just beginning. This map, together with one just begun by Hynd-Shanahan and Shanahan (2007), will prove invaluable for guiding content teachers who seek to improve their students' reading and writing in different disciplines. However, in the absence of these maps, we can learn from a number of empirical studies that have offered warrant for the idea that readers approach texts in different ways depending on the reader's purpose or goals for reading them, the reader's disciplinary commitments and practices, the nature of the text (its structure, its genre, etc.), the context in which the texts were generated, and the context in which the texts are being read.

For example, according to Samuel Wineburg (1991, 1998), who studied the reading practices of historians (and compared them to the reading practices of high school students), the same piece of historical narrative could be approached in different ways depending on the disciplinary (or other) context in which the text is being read or written. Wineburg's analysis suggests, in fact, that a text identified as a historical narrative may even lose that identity if read by someone other than an historian. Historical narrative—a primary source perhaps—could be data in the hands of a historian, literary narrative to be performed in the hands of a dramatist, literary narrative to be critiqued in the hands of a literary theorist, and interesting background information that provides context for explaining natural phenomena in the hands of a chemist (or other natural scientist).

Consequently, history educators who work from disciplinary literacy perspectives argue that deep subject matter learning in historical studies requires students to think analytically and critically about the contexts in which texts or ideas were produced. Readers must examine texts for attribution—that is, the reader must ask such questions as *Who wrote the text? What was the writer's background? What was the writer's perspective or standpoint?* Next, they ask what other sources corroborate or challenge the evidence provided from the first source (Bain, 2000; Wineburg, 1991).

Leinhardt, Stainton, and Virji (1994) argue that producing historical accounts revolves around engaging in a dialogue that considers "surviving evidence about the past and existing analytical, theoretical, and political concerns in the present" (p. 14), with the work of production depending heavily on explanation and reasoning, both of which require attention to questions of purpose, evidence, chronology, causality, and contexts. The historical process, according to Leinhardt (1994), revolves around building a compelling case or narrative that integrates evidence, chronology, and cause to both support and generate hypotheses.

Scientific literacy theorists argue, by contrast, that school science typically requires students to bring practices of prediction, observation, analysis, summarization, and presentation to their science reading (as well as to writing and oral language practices) (Lee & Fradd, 1998; Lemke, 1990). To learn science well, students of science must learn to predict explanations for natural events or phenomena; hypothesize about those predictions based on the best available information (often found in written texts); design, carry out, and record results of investigations; draw conclusions about those results in relation to their hypotheses and the existing literature; and communicate their findings to others (Blumenfeld, Marx, Patrick, & Krajcik, 1997; Hand, Wallace, & Yang, 2004; Palincsar & Magnusson, 2001; Rutherford & Ahlgren, 1990). The language of science is a specialized system that rests heavily upon themes and concepts that are not immediately apparent to a novice science learner (Eisenhart, Finkel, & Marion, 1996; Lemke, 1990). Learning science, then, means learning these themes and how to recognize them in oral and written language about the phenomenon of interest.

According to Carol Lee (2001, 2006), even the study of English literature, which often appears to draw from everyday language and "generic" literacy processes, requires yet again another set of reading skills. Reading literature revolves around interpreting figurative language and recognizing symbols, irony, and satire in texts that are situated in historical contexts, contexts of different social, cultural, and political systems. In addition to recognizing and interpreting symbols and themes in texts, students of English literature must also identify literary devices that signal emotions, motives, or goals, and develop and demonstrate an understanding of how an author constructs a world that the reader simultaneously enters and stands apart from through various narrative devices (Lee, 2005; Lee & Spratley, 2007).

Finally, in examining the literate demands in mathematics, Bass (2006) has written about the ways that mathematical understandings are intimately tied to the various texts that represent them. Bass goes so far as to claim that mathematics is completely dependent on language, arguing in fact that the very concepts of mathematics are *in the language used to express and manipulate them* (Bass, 2006, p. 3; emphasis added). Thus, the texts of mathematics depend heavily on accuracy and precision in both their production and consumption. The words, terms, symbols, and diagrams (the heart of a mathematical symbol system, according to Bass) of mathematics must be used with precision in order to generate new knowledge. Like Bass, Lemke (2003) argued that mathematics is comprised of multiple semiotic systems that both convey and produce meaning. Each of these systems can be read independently, but in mathematical reasoning these systems are typically interdependent.

What these varying takes on just the four core subject matter areas of the secondary school offer is the awareness that there are differences among the disciplines and that, for the most part, research in adolescent literacy and in the disciplines has barely begun to scratch the surface of these differences. Yore, Hand, and Prain (2002) demonstrated through interviews with practicing scientists that very few members of the disciplines are aware of their practices. Their teaching of novices typically involves apprenticeship over time, raising the question of how middle and high school teachers can apprentice novice readers and writers into subject matter reading and writing practices when they have so little daily contact with their apprentices. What's more, it is not clear whether middle and high school teachers are themselves aware of the knowledge production and communication practices of their disciplinary subject matter areas. If their teaching continues to focus on disciplinary concepts and not on practices, then are they truly engaged in responsive teaching that not only meets students' interests, but also develops and expands their skills? These questions lead to the question of what are the findings of research conducted on disciplinary literacy teaching and learning in secondary school settings?

What Does the Field Know about Literacy Pedagogy in the Subject Areas?

There are at least four perspectives on teaching and learning literacy at the secondary school level that one might consider to be a type of *disci-*

plinary literacy theory or pedagogy. An important distinction among the perspectives is that some scholars appear to conceptualize literacy as *cognitive processes*, whereas others are grounded in notions of disciplinary literacy as *cultural practices*. Another important distinction is the some perspectives focus on the people being taught, whereas others focus on the texts and language practices being taught. An interesting parallel across all the perspectives is that although they acknowledge the disciplinary subject matter being taught, they are at least as interested in the language, literacy, and thinking processes and practices used to produce and communicate knowledge in the subject areas as they are in the subject matter concepts themselves. These perspectives do not eschew the teaching of subject matter concepts, but the focus of the work is on how teaching the processes and practices of knowledge production and communication may actually better serve to teach subject matter concepts than a narrow focus on the concepts themselves.

In what follows, I briefly summarize these four perspectives on disciplinary literacy, which can be conceived of as (1) teaching cognitive literacy processes, (2) teaching epistemological processes of the disciplines, (3) teaching linguistic processes of the disciplines, and (4) teaching linguistic and discursive navigation across cultural boundaries represented in everyday life and the disciplines. For a lengthier treatment of these perspectives, see Moje (2007).

Disciplinary Literacy Pedagogy as Teaching Cognitive Literacy Processes

This category, labeled "cognitive literacy processes," has a long history of research, stemming from the content-area literacy work of Harold Herber, who promoted the idea of teaching cognitive strategies for making sense of text to adolescents as they progressed through middle and high school. For some literacy researchers and teachers, this idea was understood as *reading to learn*, and it was argued that literacy instruction needed to shift from learning to read (or write) in the lower grades to reading (or writing) to learn in the upper grades. In practice, however, the strategies developed and tested by content-area reading researchers were focused on continued development in learning to read and premised on the argument that the texts of secondary school content areas such as science, social studies, and mathematics required different kinds of reading skills from those young people had learned in earlier grades, where narrative texts dominated. A host of cognitive strategies were developed, applied, and tested in a variety of secondary school settings, such as Ogle's (1986) K–W–L (What I Know, What I Want to Know, and What I Learned) to Palincsar and Brown's (1984) reciprocal teaching and Guthrie, Wigfield, and Perencevich's (2004) Concept-Oriented Reading Instruction (CORI). These various strategies have been reviewed by a number of scholars (Alvermann & Moore, 1991; Bean, 2000; Moore & Readence, 2001; Phelps, 2005), but are not always thought of as disciplinary literacy strategies. Instead, they are conceived of as cognitive strategies for text processing, with the assumption that they can be applied to any text, whether rooted in the disciplines or found in everyday life.

As illustrated by the studies cited (see Moje, 2007, for a complete review), the primary focus of the cognitive literacy strategy research has been on the application of literacy strategies designed for elementary middle-grades learners. Many of these strategies have demonstrated promise for supporting secondary school students' comprehension of texts and have been widely recommended in reviews of useful secondary school literacy teaching strategies (Alvermann & Moore, 1991; Biancarosa & Snow; Phelps, 2005). Questions remain about the applicability of such strategies to the upper-level subject matters, however, given the specialized knowledge and literacy demands of the disciplinary domains.

One notable aspect of work in cognitive literacy strategies that has not been as well recognized is the *potential* in many of these strategies to support responsive teaching. Given the attention placed by these perspectives on readers' prior knowledge, perspective, and bias, it is appropriate to claim that, in theory, these strategies both support cognitive skill development and recognize and build on who students are as people. With more attention to how these strategies and practices should acknowledge cultural experiences and differences among readers and writers, these strategies could be leveraged to produce responsive pedagogy in the sense that they draw from students' experiences and can provide opportunities for youth to learn to independently access and evaluate texts.

What is missing, however, from the cognitive strategies work is attention to the specific demands of the practices—and thus, the texts—of the disciplines. Some scholars have acknowledged discipline-specific demands (Bulgren, Deshler, & Lenz, 2007; Conley, in press; Guthrie et al., 2004; Hynd-Shanahan & Shanahan, 2007; Schoenbach, Greenleaf, Cziko, & Hurwitz, 1999; Yore, Bisanz, & Hand, 2003; Yore & Treagust, 2006), but the studies focus more on how to develop routines among teachers to engage in text-processing strategies as a means of enhancing subject area learning. Rafaella Borasi and Marjorie Siegel's work (Borasi & Siegel, 2000; Borasi, Siegel, Fonzi, & Smith, 1998; Siegel, Borasi, & Fonzi, 1998) also connects cognitive strategies with disciplinary discourses. Borasi and Siegel describe the goal of their Reading to Learn Mathematics for Critical Thinking (RLM) research as the analysis of how and to what degree mathematics teaching and learning could be supported by the use of "rich math texts" (Borasi & Siegel, 2000, p. 9). Their idea was that text reading in mathematics could support learning and be scaffolded through the use of cognitive reading strategies designed to support students' sense making of texts. Borasi and Siegel found, however, that the reading students did depended largely on the mathematical tasks and functions for which they were engaged in reading. This work provides a useful segue to the next perspective, which focuses on how the epistemological underpinnings of a given discipline shape acts of reading, writing, and communication.

Disciplinary Literacy Pedagogy as Teaching Epistemological Processes of the Disciplines

This second group of disciplinary literacy researchers and theorists[1] reverses, in some sense, the cognitive/subject matter relationship, working within the disciplines to assess the cognition or thinking processes necessary for making sense of disciplinary texts. Following Wineburg (1991), I label this perspective the "disciplinary epistemological perspective." These research programs are less interested in generic cognitive strategies and more interested in one or more of three foci: (1) specifying the cognition of members of the disciplines as they either comprehend or produce oral and written texts (Leinhardt, 1989; VanSledright & Kelly, 1998; Wineburg, 1991; Young & Leinhardt, 1998), (2) comparing those cognitive processes of members of the disciplines to learners in the subject matter areas (Collins, Palincsar, & Magnusson, 2005; Hand, Hohenshell, & Prain, 2004; Hand, Prain, Lawrence, & Yore, 1999; Hand, Wallace, & Yang, 2004; Palincsar & Magnusson, 2001), and (3) applying those cognitive processes to educational practice (Afflerbach & VanSledright, 2001; Bain, 2000, 2006; Hynd-Shanahan, Holschuh, & Hubbard, 2004; Lee, 2005).

---

[1]These scholars do not necessarily self-identify as disciplinary literacy researchers. Indeed, they tend to operate as disciplinary specialists or as psychologists of learning. I have taken the liberty of identifying them as disciplinary literacy specialists because of their sustained attention to the texts and literate processes of the disciplines.

What is highlighted in any of those three strands is how members of a discipline *think* and how that thinking shapes the texts they produce or how they access the texts of others for disciplinary purposes, with the idea that learning how knowledge is produced and consumed within the disciplines can be applied to life as a citizen of the world. As citizens, these scholars argue, people need critical listening and reading skills to make informed decisions and critical speaking and writing skills to communicate their decisions. Informed participation in society, they argue, demands knowledge of how knowledge is produced in many domains of study. In fact, civic engagement requires not only knowledge, but also the ability to engage in the practices, if not to the level of members of the discipline, in ways that parallel those levels.

These points are especially critical when considering the critique of history and other disciplinary textbooks offered by a number of scholars. Paxton (1999), for example, has argued that the lack of authorial voice in most history textbooks produced in the United States contributes to a lack of critical reading skill on the part of adolescent (and child) history learners. Young people read history in textbooks as a series of facts rather than as a practice of constructing an evidence-based account of events shaped by author perspective, background, and temporal location. Paxton labels the lack of voice a "deafening silence" and argues that it not only produces inconsiderate text, but also makes texts less engaging to young readers. Drawing from Paxton's critique, Mimi Lee (2007) has demonstrated empirically that changes to the authorial voice of textbooks through the use of what she has developed—Visual Inquiry Texts (VIT)—can make visible the thinking that a historian might engage in around corroboration, contextualization, or sourcing of a primary source text in ways that shape students' abilities to engage in critical analysis of texts.

Palincsar and Magnusson (2001) have had similar success with the construction of a fictional scientist's notebook, written in the first person by a scientist who appears to work through the same inquiry process in which the children of Palincsar and Magnusson's project are engaged. The children read and responded to the scientist's notebook (a secondhand inquiry) throughout their own firsthand inquiry process. Palincsar and Magnusson even documented children talking back to the imaginary scientist's observations and hypotheses as recorded in their science notebooks. Without, however, access both to multiple and varied texts and to opportunities to learn to read those texts critically—as a historian, a scientist, or other disciplinarian might—young readers might not engage in critical reading and writing practices.

Similarly, Bain (2006) writes of his efforts to deconstruct the texts of his high school history classroom by teaching his students the practices of working historians. Bain also developed a computer-based scaffolding program that supported students in the process of asking sourcing, contextualizing, and corroborating questions of texts. In work beyond his own classroom, Bain has further developed and tested a classroom digital tool—the Virtual Curator and Virtual Expedition—that guides Detroit high school students as they explore museum text resources and locate relevant information (Bain & Ellenbogen, 2001). The digital tool frames students' reading and research in questions of the discipline of history (specifically in the history of the great migration and urbanization of the 20th century), and provides scaffolds that push students to pose questions and to corroborate, contextualize, and analyze the sources and information they uncover at discipline-appropriate points in their reading and narrative construction process.

In terms of disciplinary text *production*, the work of Brian Hand and colleagues (Hand et al., 1999; Hand, Wallace, & Yang, 2004) in science stands as an exemplar of the disciplinary epistemology perspective (see also Palincsar & Magnusson, 2001). Hand and colleagues began from a largely cognitive stance of applying writing strategies to the production of science texts, developing what they termed the "science writing heuristic" (SWH; Akkus, Gunel, & Hand, 2007). According to Hand and colleagues, the SWH is more than a cognitive literacy tool; rather it structures the work of writing and reasoning so that it parallels the writing and reasoning of scientists. In particular, the SWH both builds on and supports a number of features of scientific work—such as the collaborative and constructive nature of science research—as students are led through a cycle of investigation, communication of initial results, revising and clarifying claims and reasoning, and refining explanations for phenomena. In this sense, the SWH is similar to other scientific and historical explanation writing rubrics (Moje, Peek-Brown, et al., 2004; Young & Leinhardt, 1998), although Hand and colleagues (Akkus et al., 2007) argue that the SWH makes a link from the "informal, expressive writing modes that foster personally constructed science understandings and more formal, public writing modes that focus on canonical forms of reasoning in science" by guiding students through the writing of scientific reports on inquiry done in classrooms (Akkus et al., 2007).

Another version of the disciplinary epistemological perspective work draws heavily from work in the field of rhetoric and composition. This branch of work examines how writers in the disciplines and students of the disciplines make sense of their writing tasks, considering concepts such as purpose, goals, audience, and resulting form in the production of disciplinary writing (e.g., Greene, 1994; Johns & Swales, 2002; Parkinson & Adendorff, 2004). In many ways, this work closely represents that of Hand's work in disciplinary epistemology and writing. However, work informed by rhetorical perspectives operates less from a perspective that the production of disciplinary text requires knowing how members of the discipline think, and more from the perspective that regardless of discipline, a writer must understand the goals of the writing task, the perspectives and interests of the target audience, and strategies for persuasive writing in order to write a piece of text effectively.

Greene's (1994) analysis of student writers of history texts, for example, demonstrates a rhetorical take on the writing of history texts. Greene's major finding was that the context of the course shaped the students' rhetorical moves in key ways—that is, students wrote for the professor as audience, whereas the practicing historians, despite recognizing that they were playing a role in a research study, wrote for other historians in the field. With these findings, Greene underscored the importance of teaching students the rhetorical strategies in a disciplinary setting and, in particular, of attending to how those strategies can get reshaped by students' interpretation of context and audience.

Overall, one fairly common element of the disciplinary epistemological perspective of disciplinary literacy research is a focus on bringing to consciousness the cognitive work of the disciplines. However, in writing about their work from this perspective, these scholars have been less clear about the role of students' prior beliefs and practices. Each of the studies outlined here makes obvious assumptions about the skills and practices youth readers and writers do not have—that is, the skills and practices associated with the disciplines—but they say less about how they draw from students' cultural and social experiences to make connections to the disciplines. From the personal vantage point of having seen some of this work firsthand, I have seen evidence of such responsiveness in, for example, the topics studied in the scientist's journal of Palincsar and Magnusson, or the knowledge points leveraged by Bain as he draws adolescent history learners into the study of migration patterns or of what makes a great leader. But each of these studies could be more explicit about the role of responsiveness in their pedagogical practice.

In addition, although focused on reading and writing practices, by and large, work in this category does not highlight the role of language except insofar as it is necessary to learn to process the different language cues (e.g., subtexts, technical vocabulary, contextual or temporal cues, place-names) demanded by the discipline. The work of linguistic analysis is reserved for another category of disciplinary literacy pedagogy.

Disciplinary Literacy Pedagogy as Teaching Linguistic Processes of the Disciplines

This branch of disciplinary literacy pedagogy focuses squarely on language processes, at times, but not always, tied to specific disciplinary processes. In this vein, systemic functional linguistics (Halliday & Matthiessen, 2004) has gained prominence because of its precision in clarifying how subject matter learning is dependent on language. Like the cognitive research done in content literacy processes and in disciplinary learning, Coffin argues that functional linguistics seeks to "bring to consciousness (both for teachers and students) the way in which such texts are linguistically structured and shaped and the way in which writers draw on grammar and lexis (i.e., vocabulary) to create different communicative effects" (p. 414).

Schleppegrell and colleagues (Schleppegrell, 2004; Schleppegrell & Achugar, 2003; Schleppegrell, Achugar, & Oteíza, 2004) have studied the linguistic features of academic language learning and argue that academic language (oral or written), in general, is different from everyday language in terms of (1) the density of information presented, (2) the level of abstraction of concepts, (3) the technical nature of concept presentation, (4) the use of multiple semiotic systems, (5) the structural conventions, and (6) the type of voice that dominates. Scheppegrell and colleagues (Schleppegrell, 2004; Schleppegrell et al., 2004), for example, analyze textbook passages to demonstrate to history teachers how they can support students in making sense of the abstractions, multiple semiotic systems, and organizational expectations unique to history texts. According to Schleppegrell and Achugar (2003), these pedagogical moves result in increased critical reading and text comprehension among students, although specific effects are not described. Findings from a large-scale study of professional development around these linguistic techniques are in development (Schleppegrell et al., 2004).

Like the cognitive literacy and the disciplinary epistemology stances, the linguistic stance is extremely useful for highlighting the challenges of language embedded in all academic texts and the specific challenges and expectations unique to particular disciplines. Systemic functional linguistics could, however, make advances as a framework for *responsive pedagogy* if researchers attended as closely to the abstractions, density, and multiple semiotic systems of *everyday* language and texts that young people routinely use to make meaning and to claim spaces and identities (Moje, 2000).

From a linguistic standpoint, everyday texts (i.e., texts not assigned for school work) also make extensive lexical, grammatical, and structural demands on readers. Consider, for example, this text from *Lowrider Bicycle Magazine* (*www.lowriderbike.com/bike_features/03lrbsum_lowrider_bicycle_history*):

> Lowrider bikes have been around for years, although nobody has ever really pinpointed when the actual first lowrider bike hit the boulevard. Maybe the closest thing that has ever been documented was the Eddie Munster bike from the '60s TV show The Munsters, a George Barris–customized Schwinn Sting-Ray.

In this excerpt, the text can be considered high in technical language because one must know the density because of amount of information presented (from the name of the class of bicycles—which provides a cue only to those inside the discourse community of lowrider bikes—to the era in which the bikes were first documented, or to the specific type of lowrider bike mentioned in the article. The author, however, makes the concept of the lowrider bike concrete with a visual example, provided, that is, that readers are fans of, or at least familiar with, *The Munsters*. Reading on in the text, one notes the technical vocabulary and high-level everyday terms used in ways particular to the discourse community:

> Even though Schwinn and other manufacturers had discontinued their cantilever frames and started specializing in BMX bikes, there was still a market for the old classics. When Lowrider Magazine busted back out in 1988, people started to build cars as well as bikes. There were a few bikes still out there during this hibernation period, but they were cruisers and not show bikes.

In contrast to the typical voice in school textbooks, however, the authorial voice of the lowrider bike text appears casual, less distant, and less abstract, in part because of writing style. But, in fact, the text is filled with technical language and in-group references that might seem to be an abstraction to the unfamiliar reader. In other words, like school texts, the texts young people read offer abstractions, technical language, and at times dense amounts of information, rendered in a distant voice.

But their participation in the communities that produce these texts makes the texts accessible, meaningful, and engaging.

Attention to the linguistic features and demands of the texts young people read and write in homes, peer groups, families, and other settings outside of school via a functional linguistics perspective could provide an opportunity to build on young people's existing prowess with language as a way of learning academic language and text processing. Research represented in the next category of disciplinary literacy research attempts to take the cultural practices and cognitive processes of young people's everyday lives into account by explicitly drawing from and expanding those practices and processes as a way of constructing subject matter literacy practices that bridge youths' lives and the content of the subject matter areas.

Disciplinary Literacy Pedagogy as Cultural Navigation

Scholars who work from the "cultural navigation perspective" consider their work to be culturally responsive or culturally relevant pedagogy because they seek to make space for young people's everyday knowledge to be used to inform and expand mainstream academic knowledge. The theoretical basis for this work stems from the argument that the subject matter areas, or disciplines, can be viewed as spaces constructed from cultural practices just as the everyday practices of youths' lives are culturally mediated (Lee, 2001). Even more important, knowledge production in the content areas needs to be understood as the result of human interactions and practices. The disciplines are not simply bodies of knowledge to be handed down from expert to novice.

Researchers working from the cultural navigation perspective argue that part of learning in the subject matter area involves coming to understand the norms of practice for producing and communicating knowledge in the disciplines, as well as examining how subject matter norms for practice are similar to and different from everyday norms for practice. Another crucial task of subject matter education from the cultural navigation version of disciplinary literacy pedagogy is one of teaching students not only the privileged discourses of the disciplines (see Delpit, 1988), but also when and why such discourses are useful, and how these discourses and practices came to be valued. For example, in Detroit middle school science classrooms, teachers emphasize the scientific practices of data representation, analysis, and interpretation, as they teach students how to write clear scientific explanations of phenomena (Moje, Peek-Brown, et al., 2004). Even as they engage in inquiry around the phenomena, these teachers help students learn the literate practices required to make scientific investigation meaningful. Together with students, for example, they have constructed criteria for producing scientific explanations, criteria that include (1) making a claim; (2) providing multiple pieces of evidence, drawn from experimentation or the past research of others; (3) reasoning through the evidence back to the claim; and (4) writing the explanation in precise and accurate language that "anyone interested in science should be able to understand." From the cultural navigation perspective, however, what we need to continue to develop is scaffolding students' understanding of when and why they would write in "precise and accurate language" (i.e., why precision matters in the cultural practices of science) and why those explanations are not the same explanations they might give to a friend on the street (i.e., why different kinds of precision, as well as different kinds of warrant, are valued among peers in everyday interaction) (Moje, Peek-Brown, et al., 2004).

Many scholars have produced cultural navigation projects focused on disciplinary literacy with young students in classrooms across the United States (Fradd, Lee, Sutman, & Saxton, 2001; Gutiérrez, Baquedano-López, Alvarez, & Chiu, 1999; Gutiérrez, Baquedano-López, & Alvarez, 2001; Gutiérrez, Rymes, & Larson, 1995; Heath, 1983; Lee, 1999; Lee & Fradd, 1998; Moje & Hinchman, 2004; Moll, 1992; Moll & Gonzalez, 1994; Warren, Ballenger, Ogonowski, Rosebery, & Hudicourt-Barnes, 2001; Warren, Rosebery, & Conant, 1989, 1994). These are important studies that have laid the groundwork for similar work at the secondary school subject matter levels. The challenge for building on youth knowledge and connecting it to upper-grades disciplinary literacy learning, however, is not one to be underestimated. To date, the majority of the work done on connecting youths' language and literacy practices to disciplinary language and literacy practices has been done in secondary English language arts (Lee, 1993, 1995, 2001). Lee's construct of *cultural modeling* situates subject areas as cultures and seeks to tease out the demands of discourse in subject areas such as English. She then looks for spaces to link students' everyday discourses and practices specifically for the purpose of enhancing academic discourse and literate development. Studying in her own classroom, Lee demonstrated how a teacher with deep knowledge of students' backgrounds and ways with words could link those experiences and ways to the practices valued in the discipline.

In her work with Yolanda Majors (Lee & Majors, 2003), Lee maps the links between the discourse practices of a community hair salon and those of English classrooms to illustrate the possibilities for drawing on students' everyday culturally situated language, discourse, and text practices to produce socially just subject matter pedagogy. Although Lee's applications of cultural modeling have been predominantly based in the English language arts disciplines, she argues that cultural modeling—or what I am calling disciplinary literacy as cultural navigation—can be applied to any subject matter area, but will first require a mapping of both youth cultural, text-based practices and disciplinary cultural, text-based practices.

Very little work from a disciplinary literacy as cultural navigation perspective has been developed in upper-level science or mathematics. The work of Greenleaf and colleagues in WestEd (Greenleaf, Schoenbach, Cziko, & Mueller, 2001) has been promising in that regard and is especially notable because it began with a focus on cognitive literacy strategies instruction across multiple content areas and has begun to develop practices for cultural navigation as well. Similarly, although focused on younger groups of students, Warren, Rosebery, and colleagues (Rosebery, Warren, & Conant, 1992; Warren et al., 2001; Warren, Rosebery, & Conant, 1989) have developed a number of culturally responsive, language-based science teaching practices that are compelling in regard to student engagement. My own work (Moje, Collazo, Carrillo, & Marx, 2001; Moje, Ciechanowski, et al., 2004) also has sought to examine how to draw from youths' cultural backgrounds to develop deep learning of scientific concepts and literacy practices, but as we acknowledge in our attempt to "work toward" a "third space" that results from the integration of everyday and scientific knowledge, such work is in its infancy as we seek to straddle the gap between initial engagement or connection to everyday life and the distant abstractions of scientific concepts and practices from the real world of the everyday.

Robert Moses has been more successful in bridging this divide in mathematics. Cultural navigation is highly evident in the Algebra Project of Moses and colleagues (Davis & West, 2000; Moses & Cobb, 2001; West & Davis, 2004, 2005). Moses uses the term "mathematical literacy" to refer to building useable knowledge for the average citizen (rather than the elite knowledge of the mathematician). However, the work that Moses engages in with youth in the project draws on the precision of mathematical symbol systems described by Bass (2006). Indeed, the Algebra Project is unique in its ability to provide students opportunities to navigate from multiple everyday semiotic forms to multiple mathematical forms.

Although each of these projects varies in important ways in theoretical and methodological orientations, the goals of the work are similar: to provide opportunities for children and youth to bridge, navigate, and/or reconstruct both everyday and academic discourses in ways that allow them to learn disciplinary concepts and literacy skills and practices, to achieve in school settings, and to make contributions to, and changes in, society. Specifically, cultural text navigation perspectives tend to focus more on documenting and analyzing youths' text and cultural practices than do the other disciplinary literacy practices, but leave the text practices of the disciplines a bit more vague (Lee's cultural modeling and Moses's Algebra Project stand as exceptions to this critique). The disciplines are clearly acknowledged in each perspective, but close analyses are not typically offered as ways of clarifying for teachers and teacher educators how connections can be made from the everyday text practices of youths to the text practices they must engage to learn at advanced levels in the disciplines.

WHAT RESEARCH DO WE NEED?

Youth Studies

As suggested in the section on what we know about youths, adolescent and youth literacy researchers have amassed a great deal of research on the various literacy practices of particular groups of young people. In addition, national tests provide the field with information about students' literacy skills as documented on standardized instruments. We continue to need youth studies, but the work in this area could benefit from being more systematically designed to capture a wide range of youths. Ideally, federal- or foundation-level funding for the creation of adolescent literacy centers at sites across the country could be made available to study the range of texts that young people read and write, as well as the skill with which they do so. These studies would seek to rigorously and systematically document—preferably at both large and small scales—what, how, why, and when young people read and write. What's more, these collected studies could analyze the nature of texts youths read both in and out of school and document the demands of those texts and of how youths make sense of and meet those demands. Whether such funding becomes available, it would behoove adolescent literacy researchers and teachers to work together to produce global theorizations and representations of youths that draw from a number of local and particular studies.

Disciplinary Studies

In regard to the texts and practices of the disciplines, we need to follow in the footsteps of Carol Lee and Anika Spratley (2007) to chart the literacy and language practices of the disciplines in ways that are useful and accessible to educators. A fair amount of theorizing and research has been done within cognitive science and within some of the disciplines, but the field of adolescent literacy would benefit from the organized collections that document and exemplify how and why members of the disciplines read and write, and that specify how those practices might translate productively to middle and high school subject matter classrooms.

The field would also benefit from research on how teachers and students are currently using texts in subject matter classrooms. Many adolescent literacy scholars who work in teacher education programs or who conduct classroom-based research across the disciplines recognize the wide variety of approaches to using text among subject matter teachers. A large-scale study in a single discipline could demonstrate what texts get used and when, why, and how. A study that might look across subject matters and school types (i.e., urban, rural, suburban; middle class, working class, high poverty) would also provide compelling information. Multiplying such studies, and bringing them together in an integrated fashion to offer an empirically based representation of text use in secondary school settings, would have a great deal to say to the field and to policymakers and professional developers.

Disciplinary Literacy Studies

To expand the research we already have on various perspectives on disciplinary literacy—perspectives that could be productively integrated to produce truly responsive secondary subject matter literacy teaching and learning—we need to continue research on interventions such as those represented in the work of the researcher and teachers reviewed in earlier sections of this chapter. Each of these scholars works to teach adolescents to make sense of and produce the texts of their disciplines, starting first with who those young people are, revealing what the disciplines demand of them as readers and writers, and then employing various cognitive, linguistic, and rhetorical strategies to help youths make sense of texts. However, we need to develop ways to carefully document not only the enactments of these different disciplinary literacy teaching practices, but also their outcomes. Ideally, studies would include systematic qualitative analyses of young people's growth over time in terms of skill and attitude, as well as quantifiable effects of improvements to skill and attitude.

Disciplinary Literacy Teacher Education Studies

Finally, we need to begin to study preservice and inservice teacher learning to engage in responsive disciplinary literacy pedagogy. We need to understand what teachers believe about their disciplines and how those disciplinary subcultures and commitments may shape their practice, especially in regard to teaching from, with, and to texts (see O'Brien, Stewart, & Moje, 1995). We need to document how different teacher education programs are attempting to restructure their work to integrate disciplinary literacy teaching—as represented by an amalgam of perspectives in this review—across their programs. And we need to ask what else we need to do in preservice and inservice teacher education to foster an awareness of the role of text, language, and literacy in responsive teaching across the disciplinary subject areas of secondary schools?

In sum, we need concerted and integrated efforts at many levels in secondary subject matter literacy teaching if such teaching is to become responsive to its constituents by not only recognizing and valuing who they are, but helping them become critically literate, strategic adults who not only possess knowledge of the disciplines, but also know how it was produced and can participate in that production in the future.

REFERENCES

Afflerbach, P., & VanSledright, B. (2001). Hath! Doth! Middle graders reading innovative history text. *Journal of Adolescent and Adult Literacy, 44*(8), 696–707.

Akkus, R., Gunel, M., & Hand, B. (2007). Comparing an inquiry based approach known as the science writing heuristic to traditional science teaching practices: Are there differences? *iFirst International Journal of Science Education*, pp. 1–21.

Alvermann, D. E. (2001). Reading adolescents' reading identities: Looking back to see ahead. *Journal of Adolescent and Adult Literacy, 44*, 676–690.

Alvermann, D. E., & Moore, D. W. (1991). Secondary school reading. In R. Barr, M. L. Kamil, P. B. Mosenthal, & P. D. Pearson (Eds.), *Handbook of reading research* (Vol. 2, pp. 951–983). New York: Longman.

American College Testing Service. (2006). Retrieved August 15, 2006, from *www.act.org/path/policy/pdf/reading_report.pdf*

Andrews, V. C. (1979). *Flowers in the attic.* New York: Simon & Schuster.

Bain, R. (2000). Into the breach: Using research and theory to shape history instruction. In P. Seixas, P. Stearns, & S. Wineberg (Eds.), *Teaching, learning and knowing history: National and international perspectives* (pp. 331–353). New York: New York University Press.

Bain, R. (2006). Rounding up unusual suspects: Facing the authority hidden in the history classroom. *Teachers College Record, 108*(10), 2080–2114.

Bain, R. B., & Ellenbogen, K. M. (2001). Placing objects within disciplinary perspectives: Examples from history and science. In S. Paris (Ed.), *Perspectives on object-centered learning in museums* (pp. 153–170). Hillsdale, NJ: Erlbaum.

Bass, H. (2006, March). *What is the role of oral and written language in knowledge generation in mathematics?* Paper presented at the Adolescent Literacy symposium, University of Michigan.

Bean, T. (2000). Reading in the content areas: Social constructivist dimensions. In M. L. Kamil, P. B. Mosenthal, P. D. Pearson, & R. Barr (Eds.), *Handbook of reading research* (Vol. 3, pp. 629–644). Mahwah, NJ: Erlbaum.

Biancarosa, G., & Snow, C. E. (2004). *Reading next—A vision for action and research in middle and high school literacy. A report to the Carnegie Corporation of New York.* Washington, DC: Alliance for Excellent Education.

Blumenfeld, P. C., Marx, R. W., Patrick, H., & Krajcik, J. S. (1997). Teaching for understanding. In B. J. Biddle, T. L. Good, & I. F. Goodson (Eds.), *International handbook of teachers and teaching* (pp. 819–878). Dordrecht, The Netherlands: Kluwer Academic.

Borasi, R., & Siegel, M. (2000). *Reading counts: Expanding the role of reading in mathematics classrooms.* New York: Teachers College Press.

Borasi, R., Siegel, M., Fonzi, J., & Smith, C. (1998). Using transactional reading strategies to support sense-making and discussions in mathematics classrooms. *Journal for Research in Mathematics Education, 29*(3), 275–305.

Bulgren, J., Deshler, D. D., & Lenz, B. K. (2007). Engaging adolescents with learning disabilities in higher-order thinking about history concepts. *Journal of Learning Disabilities, 40*, 121–133.

Camitta, M. (1993). Vernacular writing: Varieties of literacy among Philadelphia high school students. In B. V. Street (Ed.), *Cross-cultural approaches to literacy* (pp. 228–246). Cambridge, UK: Cambridge University Press.

Canfield, J., Hansen, M. V., & Kirberger, K. (1997). *Chicken soup for the teenage soul: 101 stories of life, love, and learning.* Deerfield Beach, FL: Health Communications.

Chandler-Olcott, K., & Mahar, D. (2003). "Tech-savviness" meets multiliteracies: Exploring adolescent girls' technology-mediated literacy practices. *Reading Research Quarterly, 38*(3), 356–385.

Ciechanowski, K. M., & Moje, E. B. (2002, December). *Youth literacy and language practices in the enactment of identity.* Paper presented at the National Reading Conference, Miami, FL.

Collins, K. M., Palincsar, A. S., & Magnusson, S. J. (2005). Science for all: A discursive analysis examining teacher support of student thinking in inclusive classrooms. In R. Yerrick & W.-M. Roth (Eds.), *Establishing scientific classroom discourse communities: Multiple voices of teaching and learning research* (pp. 199–224). Mahwah, NJ: Erlbaum.

Conley, M. (in press). Improving adolescent comprehension: Developing comprehension strategies in the content areas. In S. E. Israel & G. G. Duffy (Eds.), *Handbook of research on reading comprehension*. New York: Erlbaum.

Cowan, P. M. (2005). Putting it out there: Revealing Latino visual discourse in the Hispanic academic summer program for middle school students. In B. V. Street (Ed.), *Literacies across educational contexts: Mediating learning and teaching* (pp. 145–169). Philadelphia: Caslon.

Cuauhtemoc Sanchez, C. (1995). *La ultima oportunidad*. Mexico City, Mexico: Ediciones Selectas Diamantes.

Davis, F. E., & West, M. M. (2000). *The impact of the Algebra Project on mathematics achievement*. Cambridge, MA: Program Evaluation and Research Group, Lesley College.

Donahue, P., Daane, M., & Grigg, W. (2003). *The nation's report card: Reading highlights 2003* (NCES 2004–452). Washington, DC: U.S. Government Printing Office.

Eisenhart, M., Finkel, E., & Marion, S. F. (1996). Creating conditions for scientific literacy: A re-examination. *American Educational Research Journal, 33*(2), 261–295.

Finders, M. J. (1997). *Just girls: Hidden literacies and life in junior high*. New York: Teachers College Press.

Fradd, S. H., Lee, O., Sutman, F. X., & Saxton, M. K. (2001). Promoting science literacy with English language learners through instructional materials development: A case study. *Bilingual Research Journal, 25*(4), 479–501.

Friedman, T. L. (2005). *The world is flat: A brief history of the 21st century*. New York: Farrar, Strauss, & Giroux.

Gates, B. (2005). Remarks at the National Governor's Association National Education Summit on high school. Retrieved June 1, 2006, from *www.gatesfoundation.org/ MediaCenter/Speeches/BillgSpeeches/BGSpeechNGA-050226.htm*

Gee, J. P. (1996). *Social linguistics and literacies: Ideology in discourses* (2nd ed.). London: Falmer.

Greene, S. (1994). Students as authors in the study of history. In G. Leinhardt, I. L. Beck, & C. Stainton (Eds.), *Teaching and learning in history* (pp. 137–171). Hillsdale, NJ: Erlbaum.

Greenleaf, C., Schoenbach, R., Cziko, C., & Mueller, F. L. (2001). Apprenticing adolescent readers to academic literacy. *Harvard Educational Review, 71*(1), 79–129.

Gustavson, L. (2007). *Youth learning on their own terms*. New York: Routledge.

Guthrie, J. T., Wigfield, A., & Perencevich, K. C. (2004). *Motivating reading comprehension: Concept-oriented reading instruction*. Mahwah, NJ: Erlbaum.

Gutiérrez, K. D., Baquedano-Lopez, P., & Alvarez, H. H. (2001). Literacy as hybridity: Moving beyond bilingualism in urban classrooms. In M. de la Luz Reyes & J. J. Halcon (Eds.), *The best for our children: Critical perspectives on literacy for Latino students. Language and literacy series* (pp. 122–141). New York: Teachers College Press.

Gutiérrez, K. D., Baquedano-López, P., Alvarez, H., & Chiu, M. M. (1999). Building a culture of collaboration through hybrid language practices. *Theory into Practice, 38*(2), 87–93.

Gutiérrez, K. D., Rymes, B., & Larson, J. (1995). Script, counterscript, and underlife in the classroom: James Brown versus Brown v. Board of Education. *Harvard Educational Review, 65*, 445–471.

Halliday, M. A. K., & Matthiessen, C. M. I. M. (2004). *An introduction to functional grammar* (3rd ed.). London: Arnold.

Hand, B., Hohenshell, L., & Prain, V. (2004). Exploring students' responses to conceptual questions when engaged with planned writing experiences: A study with year 10 science students. *Journal of Research in Science Teaching, 41*, 186–210.

Hand, B., Prain, V., Lawrence, C., & Yore, L. D. (1999). A writing in science framework designed to enhance science literacy. *International Journal of Science Education, 21*(10), 1021–1035.

Hand, B., Wallace, C., & Yang, E. (2004). Using the science writing heuristic to enhance learning outcomes from laboratory activities in seventh grade science: Quantitative and qualitative aspects. *International Journal of Science Education, 26*, 131–149.

Heath, S. B. (1983). *Ways with words: Language, life, and work in communities and classrooms.* Cambridge, UK: Cambridge University Press.

Herber, H. (1978). *Teaching reading in the content areas.* Englewood Cliffs, NJ: Prentice-Hall.

Hinton, S. E. (1967). *The outsiders.* New York: Viking Press.

Hynd-Shanahan, C., Holschuh, J. P., & Hubbard, B. P. (2004). Thinking like a historian: College students' reading of multiple historical documents. *Journal of Literacy Research, 36*(2), 141–176.

Hynd-Shanahan, C., & Shanahan, T. (2007). *Content area reading/learning: Flexibility in knowledge acquisition.* Unpublished manuscript.

Ingalls, R. L. (2005). *Taking a page from their books: Negotiating containment and resuscitating rhetoric in writing across academic and spoken-work genres.* Unpublished doctoral dissertation, University of Michigan, Ann Arbor.

Johns, A. M., & Swales, J. M. (2002). Literacy and disciplinary practices: Opening and closing perspectives. *Journal of English for Academic Purposes, 1*, 13–28.

Lam, W. S. E. (2004). Border discourses and identities in transnational youth culture. In J. Mahiri (Ed.), *What they don't learn in school* (pp. 79–97). New York: Lang.

Leander, K. M., & Lovvorn, J. (2006). Literacy networks: Following the circulation of texts, bodies, and objects in the schooling and online gaming of one youth. *Cognition and Instruction, 24*(3), 291–340.

Lee, C. D. (1993). *Signifying as a scaffold for literary interpretation: The pedagogical implications of an African American discourse genre* (NCTE Research Report No. 26). Urbana, IL: National Council of Teachers of English.

Lee, C. D. (1995). A culturally based cognitive apprenticeship: Teaching African American high school students skills in literary interpretation. *Reading Research Quarterly, 30*(4), 608–630.

Lee, C. D. (2001). Is October Brown Chinese?: A cultural modeling activity system for underachieving students. *American Educational Research Journal, 38*(1), 97–141.

Lee, C. D. (2005, December). *Re-conceptualizing disciplinary literacies and the adolescent struggling reader: Placing culture at the forefront.* Paper presented at the annual meeting of the National Reading Conference.

Lee, C. D. (2006). Every good-bye ain't gone: Analyzing the cultural underpinnings of classroom talk. *Qualitative Studies in Education, 19*, 305–327.

Lee, C. D., & Majors, Y. (2003). Heading up the street: Localized opportunities for shared constructions of knowledge. *Pedagogy, Culture and Society, 11*(1), 49–68.

Lee, C. D., & Spratley, A. (2007). *Reading in the disciplines and the challenges of adolescent literacy* (A report to the Carnegie Corporation of New York). New York: Carnegie Corporation of New York.

Lee, M. (2007). *Promoting historical inquiry using secondary sources.* Unpublished doctoral dissertation, University of Michigan, Ann Arbor.

Lee, O. (1999). Science knowledge, world views, and information sources in social and cultural contexts: Making sense after a natural disaster. *American Educational Research Journal, 36*(2), 187–219.

Lee, O., & Fradd, S. H. (1998). Science for all, including students from non-English language backgrounds. *Educational Researcher, 27*(3), 12–21.

Leinhardt, G. (1989). Math lessons: A contrast of novice and expert competence. *Journal of Research in Mathematics Education, 20*, 52–75.

Leinhardt, G. (1994). History: A time to be mindful. In G. Leinhardt, I. L. Beck, & C. Stainton (Eds.), *Teaching and learning in history* (pp. 209–255). Hillsdale, NJ: Erlbaum.

Leinhardt, G., Stainton, C., & Virji, S. M. (1994). A sense of history. *Educational Psychologist, 29*(2), 79–88.

Lemke, J. L. (1990). *Talking science: Language, learning, and values.* Norwood, NJ: Ablex.

Lemke, J. L. (2003). Mathematics in the middle: Measure, picture, gesture, sign, and word. In M. Anderson, A. Saenz-Ludlow, S. Zellweger, & V. V. Cifarelli (Eds.), *Educational perspective on mathematics as semiosis: From thinking to interpreting to knowing* (pp. 215–234). Ottawa, ON, Canada: Legas.

Lewis, C., & Fabos, B. (2005). Instant messaging, literacies, and social identities. *Reading Research Quarterly, 40*(4), 470–501.

Mahiri, J. (Ed.). (2003). *What they don't learn in school: Literacy in the lives of urban youth.* New York: Lang.

Moje, E. B. (2000). To be part of the story: The literacy practices of gangsta adolescents. *Teachers College Record, 102*, 652–690.

Moje, E. B. (2007). Developing socially just subject-matter instruction: A review of the literature on disciplinary literacy. In L. Parker (Ed.), *Review of research in education* (pp. 1–44). Washington, DC: American Educational Research Association.

Moje, E. B., Collazo, T., Carrillo, R., & Marx, R. W. (2001). "Maestro, what is 'quality'?": Language, literacy, and discourse in project-based science. *Journal of Research in Science Teaching, 38*(4), 469–496.

Moje, E. B., & Hinchman, K. A. (2004). Culturally responsive practices for youth literacy learning. In T. L. Jetton & J. A. Dole (Eds.), *Adolescent literacy research and practice* (pp. 331–350). New York: Guilford Press.

Moje, E. B., Overby, M., Tysvaer, N., & Morris, K. (in press). The complex world of adolescent literacy: Myths, motivations, and mysteries. *Harvard Educational Review.*

Moje, E. B., Peek-Brown, D., Sutherland, L. M., Marx, R. W., Blumenfeld, P., & Krajcik, J. (2004). Explaining explanations: Developing scientific literacy in middle-school project-based science reforms. In D. Strickland & D. E. Alvermann (Eds.), *Bridging the gap: Improving literacy learning for preadolescent and adolescent learners in grades 4–12* (pp. 227–251). New York: Carnegie Corporation.

Moll, L. C. (1992). Literacy research in community and classrooms: A sociocultural approach. In R. Beach, J. L. Green, M. L. Kamil, & T. Shanahan (Eds.), *Multidisciplinary perspectives in literacy research* (pp. 211–244). Urbana, IL: National Conference on Research in English and National Council of Teachers of English.

Moll, L. C., & Gonzalez, N. (1994). Critical issues: Lessons from research with language-minority children. *Journal of Reading Behavior, 26*(4), 439–456.

Moore, D. W., & Readence, J. E. (2001). Situating secondary school literacy research. In E. B. Moje & D. G. O'Brien (Eds.), *Constructions of literacy: Studies of teaching and learning in and out of secondary schools* (pp. 3–25). Mahwah, NJ: Earlbaum.

Moses, R., & Cobb, C. E. (2001). *Radical equations: Civil rights from Mississippi to the Algebra Project.* Boston: Beacon Press.

National Endowment for the Arts. (2004). *Reading at risk: A survey of literary reading in America* (No. 46). Washington, DC: National Endowment for the Arts.

O'Brien, D. G., Stewart, R. A., & Moje, E. B. (1995). Why content literacy is difficult to infuse into the secondary school: Complexities of curriculum, pedagogy, and school culture. *Reading Research Quarterly, 30,* 442–463.

O'Connor, S. (1996). *Will my name be shouted out?: Reaching inner city students through the power of writing.* New York: Touchstone.

Ogle, D. M. (1986). K–W–L: A teaching model that develops active reading of expository text. *Reading Teacher, 39,* 564–570.

Palincsar, A. S., & Brown, A. L. (1984). Reciprocal teaching of comprehension fostering and comprehension-monitoring activities. *Cognition and Instruction, 1*(2), 117–175.

Palincsar, A. S., & Magnusson, S. J. (2001). The interplay of first-hand and text-based investigations to model and support the development of scientific knowledge and reasoning. In S. M. Carver & D. Klahr (Eds.), *Cognition and instruction: 25 years of progress* (pp. 152–193). Mahwah, NJ: Erlbaum.

Parkinson, J., & Adendorff, R. (2004). The use of popular science articles in teaching scientific literacy. *English for Specific Purposes, 23,* 379–396.

Paxton, R. J. (1999). A deafening silence: History textbooks and the students who read them. *Review of Educational Research, 69*(3), 315–339.

Perie, M., Grigg, W. S., & Donahue, P. L. (2005). *The nation's report card: Reading 2005* (NCES 2006-451). Washington, DC: U.S. Government Printing Office.

Phelps, S. F. (2005). *Ten years of research on adolescent literacy, 1994–2004: A review* (ED-01-CO-0011). Naperville, IL: Learning Point Associates.

Rosebery, A., Warren, B., & Conant, F. (1992). Appropriating scientific discourse: Findings from language minority classrooms. *Journal of the Learning Sciences, 2*(1), 1–04.

Rowling, J. K. (1999). *Harry Potter and the prisoner of Azkaban.* New York: Arthur A. Levine/Scholastic Books.

Rutherford, F. J., & Ahlgren, A. (1990). *Science for all Americans.* New York: Oxford University Press.

Schleppegrell, M. J. (2004). *The language of schooling: A functional linguistics perspective.* Mahwah, NJ: Erlbaum.

Schleppegrell, M. J., & Achugar, M. (2003). Learning language and learning history: A functional linguistics approach. *TESOL Journal, 12*(2), 21–27.

Schleppegrell, M. J., Achugar, M., & Oteíza, T. (2004). The grammar of history: Enhancing content-based instruction through a functional focus on language. *TESOL Quarterly, 38*(1), 67–93.

Schoenbach, R., Greenleaf, C., Cziko, C., & Hurwitz, L. (1999). *Reading for understanding: A guide to improving reading in middle and high school classrooms.* San Francisco: Jossey-Bass.

Shuman, A., & Blue, B. (1999). Ethnography of writing. In D. A. Wagner, R. L. Venezky, & B. V. Street (Eds.), *Literacy: An international handbook* (pp. 107–112). Boulder, CO: Westview Press.

Siegel, M., Borasi, R., & Fonzi, J. (1998). Supporting students' mathematical inquiries through reading. *Journal for Research in Mathematics Education, 29*(4), 378–413.

Stanley, J. (2003). Practicing for romance: Adolescent girls read the romance novel. In J. Mahiri (Ed.), *What they don't learn in school: Literacy in the lives of urban youth* (pp. 169–180). New York: Lang.

VanDerPloeg, L. S. (2006). *Reading race: A study of literacy, race and ethnicity in the ELA classroom.* Unpublished doctoral dissertation, University of Michigan, Ann Arbor.

VanDerPloeg, L. S., & Moje, E. B. (2004, December). *Urban youth reading for "real": Intersections of race, ethnicity, relationships, and urban experience.* Paper presented at the National Reading Conference, San Antonio, TX.

VanSledright, B. A., & Kelly, C. (1998). Reading American history: The influence of multiple sources on six fifth graders. *Elementary School Journal, 98,* 239–265.

Warren, B., Ballenger, C., Ogonowski, M., Rosebery, A., & Hudicourt-Barnes, J. (2001). Rethinking diversity in learning science: The logic of everyday languages. *Journal of Research in Science Teaching, 38,* 1–24.

Warren, B., Rosebery, A., & Conant, F. (1989). *Cheche Konnen: Science and literacy in language minority classrooms* (Report No. 7305). Cambridge, MA: Bolt, Beranek & Newman.

Warren, B., Rosebery, A., & Conant, F. (1994). Discourse and social practice: Learning science in a language minority classroom. In D. Spener (Ed.), *Adult biliteracy in the United States* (pp. 191–210). Washington, DC: Center for Applied Linguistics.

West, M. M., & Davis, F. E. (2004). *The Algebra Project at Lanier High School, Jackson, MS: Implementation and student outcomes.* Cambridge, MA: Lesley College, Program Evaluation and Research Group.

West, M. M., & Davis, F. E. (2005). *Research related to the Algebra Project's intervention to improve student learning in mathematics: Report to State of Virginia Department of Education.* Cambridge, MA: Lesley University, Program Evaluation and Research Group.

Wineburg, S. S. (1991). On the reading of historical texts: Notes on the breach between school and the academy. *American Educational Research Journal, 28*(3), 495–519.

Wineburg, S. S. (1998). Reading Abraham Lincoln: An expert/expert study in the interpretation of historical texts. *Cognitive Science, 22*(3), 319–346.

Yore, L. D., Bisanz, G. L., & Hand, B. M. (2003). Examining the literacy component of science literacy: 25 years of language arts and science research. *International Journal of Science Education, 25*(6), 689–725.

Yore, L. D., Hand, B. M., & Prain, V. (2002). Scientists as writers. *Science Education, 10,* 672–692.

Yore, L. D., & Treagust, D. F. (2006). Current realities and future possibilities: Language and science literacy—Empowering research and informing instruction. *International Journal of Science Education, 28*(2–3), 291–314.

Young, K. M., & Leinhardt, G. (1998). Writing from primary documents: A way of knowing in history. *Written Communication, 15*(1), 25.

5

Strategies That Improve Adolescents' Performance with Content-Area Texts

MARK W. CONLEY
JOSEPH R. FREIDHOFF
KRISTINE GRITTER
DEBORAH VRIEND VAN DUINEN

The interest in improving adolescent literacy has prompted a groundswell of authoritative panel reports (Berman & Biancarosa, 2005; National Association of Secondary School Principals, 2005; National Association of State Boards of Education, 2005), official government documents (U.S. Department of Education, 2007), and research reviews (Biancarosa & Snow, 2004; Graham & Perin, 2007). With the exception of *Writing Next*, a research review on writing instruction, few of these reports are based on any kind of rigorous review of research comparable to *Preventing Reading Difficulties in Young Children* (Snow, Burns, & Griffin, 1998) or the National Reading Panel's *Report* (2000). Often such reports or similar documents claiming a research base are written by panels featuring researchers whose expertise is in literacy for young children rather than literacy for adolescents. Despite a lack of grounding in actual research evidence, many of these reports garner much credibility in the field. Their calls to action may be based on flimsy evidence. This, then, is an important problem to address.

One particular area of concern involves calls for strategies to improve adolescents' comprehension of content-area texts. For example, the report from the National Association of State Boards of Education calls for professional development in "research-based literacy strategies" to provide effective content-based instruction (National Association of State Boards of Education, 2005). However, achieving such a goal is complicated by confusion as to what exactly constitutes a "strategy." In some cases, the term is used to describe what teachers do to facilitate understanding of content-area texts. In other cases, it is used to characterize what adolescents should learn to do to facilitate their own understanding of content-area texts. Rarely, if ever, do these reports make connections between the instructional strategies teachers use in the classroom—teaching strategies—and the development of skills that students employ—comprehension strategies—to make sense of content-area texts (Conley, 2008).

The purpose of this chapter is to review the research on strategies adolescents can use for comprehending content-area texts. The work reported here is part of a year-long review of adolescent literacy research with a focus on interventions and literacy outcomes. The review procedures have been modeled after those used for the National Reading Panel's *Report*, including database searches, use of search engines, specific journal searches, contact with relevant professional organizations, and contacts with experts in various fields of study, including the content-area disciplines. In this chapter, we examine effective interventions for whole classrooms, struggling adolescent readers, the content areas, and online learning environments, all on behalf of adolescent development of comprehension strategies.

ADOLESCENTS AND COMPREHENSION STRATEGIES IN WHOLE CLASSROOMS

Classrooms full of adolescents are complex literacy environments. Secondary classrooms can encompass a very diverse mix of very able readers and writers and struggling readers or writers. To make matters even more complex, there are times when very capable readers or writers struggle with literacy while struggling readers or writers demonstrate moments of startlingly proficient literacy performance. Thus, while the reality of who struggles and why changes from moment to moment, from text to text, and from assignment to assignment, teachers must continually strive to reach the capable as well as the struggling adolescent—and all the students in between. As such, an important question is: "What literacy strategies, instructional practices, and interventions work for the range of adolescents within a secondary classroom?"

Research that answers this question is rare. The National Reading Panel's *Report* in 2000 found a scientific basis for seven comprehension strategies. However, 76% of the studies for the basis of the report on text comprehension were conducted in grades three through six (National Reading Panel, 2000). Few of the studies in the National Reading Panel's *Report* were conducted in content areas such as science, mathematics, social studies, or English. Most of the research on comprehension strategy instruction has been conducted in relatively simple domains requiring basic recall or summarization tasks (Pressley & Hilden, 2006). As a result, very little is known about the teaching or the application of comprehension strategies for adolescents in content-area classrooms.

In our literature review, we looked at five well-regarded literacy journals for evidence of successful comprehension interventions. The journals were *Research in the Teaching of English, Reading Research and Instruction, Reading Research Quarterly,* the *Journal of Adolescent and Adult Literacy,* and the *Journal of Literacy Research.* Two databases, ERIC and PsychInfo, were reviewed, covering the past 5 years (2001–2006), to find research on comprehension strategies, instructional practices, and interventions that work for entire classrooms. Based on input from a group of literacy researchers, we employed the following 14 phrases in locating research for this review: "reading disability interventions," "reading strategies," "reading instruction," "reading outcomes," "reading achievement," "intervention strategies," "intervention outcomes," "academic achievement," "academic outcomes," "academic growth," "achievement gap," "performance gap," "intervention protocols," and "reading intervention protocols."

Thousands of research articles appeared after employing these phrases to search the journals and the indexes. Follow-up criteria adapted from the National Reading Panel's *Report* were used to further select studies. Inclusion criteria consisted of the following. The study:

- Was conducted in intact classroom groups (not pull-out programs or small groups) consisting of students representing a range of abilities.
- Included adolescents (sixth- through 12th-grade students).
- Incorporated a pre- and postdesign to measure intervention or strategy effectiveness.

An article did not have to include a control group to be considered for this analysis. Only seven articles met the inclusion requirements in selected journals from the past 5 years.

Several issues emerge when reviewing the literacy interventions, methodologies, and findings of this scant body of research. First, and perhaps most obvious, secondary classrooms are overlooked in literacy research, in comparison with research in elementary classrooms. Second, little attention is paid to student diversity and ability within the existing adolescent research. Little, if any, information is provided regarding the characteristics of adolescents in each of the studies. This is surprising given the research reviews in adolescent literacy concerned with issues of adolescent identity, motivation, and multiple literacies (Alvermann, Hinchman, Moore, Phelps, & Waff, 2006). Third, there is very little consistency across adolescent literacy research with regards to the measurement of the effectiveness of literacy strategies, instructional practices, and intervention outcomes. Interventions in this analysis varied widely, as did participant age or grade, measurement tools, and length of implementation. In many cases a plethora of interventions were used (as would be expected for research that takes place in complicated, naturalistic environments), making informed interpretation of outcome measures murky at best. There is a great need for more purposeful quantitative and qualitative research on effective classroom adolescent literacy practices—research that informs teachers about the kinds of adolescents involved in the research, research that can be replicated across classrooms and can establish a corpus of adolescent research, and research that deals with the very real literacy struggles of adolescents and their teachers.

STRUGGLING ADOLESCENT READERS AND COMPREHENSION STRATEGIES

The "struggling adolescent reader" is a contentious term. There are lots of commonly applied labels within the research: "slow readers," "disabled readers," "low-achieving readers," "remedial readers," and "readers with learning disabilities." The term "struggling" can refer to students with clinically diagnosed reading disabilities as well as to those who are unmotivated, disenchanted, or generally unsuccessful. The label takes on different characteristics depending on who is defining it (Moore et al., 2000). However, despite the debate over who is or who is not struggling, research has repeatedly shown that a significant proportion of adolescents experience reading difficulties. For example, the 2003 National Assessment of Educational Progress found that in the eighth grade, 31% of boys and 21% of girls could not read at the basic literacy level (Snow & Biancarosa, 2003).

For this review of research on struggling readers, the following search phrases were used: "adolescents," "secondary education," "secondary school education," "secondary students," "high school students," "high school education," "middle school students," "middle school," "remedial," "reading," "reading failure," "reading difficulties," "reading difficulty," "reading improvement," "reading disabilities," "corrective reading," "special education," "learning disabilities," "emotional disturbances," "special needs students," "reading instruction," "reading strategies," "reading interventions," "instructional effectiveness," "reading research," "oral reading," "reading ability," "reading comprehension," "phonological awareness," "word recognition," "sight reading," "reading accuracy," "reading fluency," and "phonology." Journals reviewed included the *Journal of Learning Disabilities, Remedial and Special Education, Learning Disability Quarterly, Learning Disabilities Research and Practice, Exceptional Children*, the *Journal of Special Education, Reading Improvement*, the *Journal of Adolescent and Adult Literacy, Reading Research and Instruction, Education and Treatment of Children, School Psychology Review*, and the *Journal of Behavioral Education*. Search terms and journals were recommended by experts on struggling adolescents in literacy and special education.

Twenty-one studies were identified as meeting the criteria of focusing on adolescent struggling readers. A vast majority of the research on struggling readers examines early intervention from kindergarten through grade three. Much of this research is conducted in special education classrooms, though some is also conducted in regular education classrooms. Most occur in English or language arts classrooms with somewhat less research happening in mathematics, science, or social studies classrooms. Much of this research comes from the University of Kansas Center for Research on Learning.

The research on struggling adolescent readers emphasizes many different kinds of interventions. Some interventions stress teacher change, such as getting teachers to think differently about content and pedagogy. An exemplar of this research concerns content enhancement routines (Bulgren, Deshler, & Lenz, 2007). Another intervention priority is to teach students how to acquire and use learning strategies (Deshler et al., 2001). Yet intervention research does not present a clear pattern for what instruction would be best for struggling readers. Intervention programs that target one aspect of comprehension may result in improved comprehension skills, but only for specific materials (Mastropiere et al., 2001). Sometimes an intervention is shown to improve one aspect of reading and not others. For example, Valleley and Shriver (2003) found that repeated readings helped students' fluency but not their comprehension. A critical question for intervention research concerns whether specific kinds of intervention actually reduce the gap between struggling readers and their more successful peers (Calhoon, 2005).

Generally, studies on struggling adolescent readers are short in duration, ranging from several 50-minute sessions in some studies to year-long investigations in others. This makes it difficult at best to draw any conclusions about the long-term effects of any intervention. Many rely almost exclusively on standardized tests as opposed to evaluating performance on classroom or state assessments. Researchers may not be fully capturing what students are learning.

Some of the research on struggling readers is open to criticism for being too narrow. Rarely are issues of motivation or authentic texts, tasks, or contexts seriously considered. For example, Manset-Williams and Nelson (2005) raise the dilemma of balancing the need for explicit instruction with the authenticity of the reading experience. The more explicit and direct the instruction, the less authentic and more contrived the reading experience may be (Manset-Williams & Nelson, 2005). With an optimal degree of explicitness in comprehension instruction, the experience of reading can become less generalizable to multiple situations, a common problem for adolescents moving from one content area to another in a school day.

LEARNING WITH TEXTS IN THE CONTENT AREAS: MATHEMATICS AND SCIENCE

One of the first dilemmas in reviewing research in the content areas with regard to texts and comprehension strategies is that the term "comprehension" rarely appears in many of the disciplinary journals. Therefore, recognized researchers in the disciplines were consulted with regard to key phrases that would signal comprehension activities within the disciplines. For mathematics, key phrases included "problem solving," "mathematical reasoning," and "mathematical thinking." Mathematics education journals recommended by the experts included the *Journal for Research in Mathematics Education, School Science and Mathe-*

matics, and *Educational Studies in Mathematics*. In science, key terms included "inquiry-based reasoning" and "model-based reasoning." Recommended journals included the *Journal for Research in Science Teaching*, *Science Education*, and the *International Journal of Science Education*. Of course, the search terms identified are not exactly the same as "comprehension," and thus any conclusions drawn from this review are subject to interpretation.

Thirty studies were identified in mathematics education and 63 studies were identified in science education through using the key search terms and going back 5 years through the literature. These studies represented a highly diverse range of learning problems, opportunities, and contexts within both disciplines.

The history of research in adolescent literacy and content-area literacy has been to offer up generic approaches to issues of activating prior knowledge, fluency, comprehension, writing, and assessment. As Figure 5.1 illustrates, generic approaches may not be sufficient to address the particular demands of learning from texts in mathematics and science. Several examples from the research illustrate the gap between what content-area literacy/adolescent literacy research offers and the particulars of learning in the disciplines.

A line of research within mathematics education concerns how adolescents learn to solve authentic mathematical tasks. In one study, seventh graders were taught to formulate and answer four kinds of questions (Kramarski, Mevarech, & Arami, 2002):

- Comprehension—asking questions that help readers reflect on and analyze a problem before solving it..
- Connection—asking questions about similarities and differences with other problems.
- Strategic—asking questions about strategies that might be appropriate in solving a problem.
- Reflection—asking "Does this make sense?" and "How can I verify my solution?"

Students who were taught to ask these questions were much more effective at solving authentic problems in comparison with students who did not know how to ask these questions.

There is an equally visible line of research in literacy about asking questions, such as with question–answer relationships (Raphael & Pearson, 1985). This approach helps students relate questions to the sources of information for their responses. As effective as this approach

Mathematics education	Science education
Cognitive conflict and inferential reasoning	Cognitive conflict
Problem solving	Building knowledge and argumentation skills
Errors in linear reasoning	Graphicacy
Constructing views of data	Metacognition in chemistry
Developing mathematical thinking	Computer-simulated learning
Improving graph interpretation	Developing mental modeling
Developing mathematical discourse	Predictors of problem solving
Comprehension reflected in mathematics testing	Project-based science curricula and achievement
Effects of changes in scale	Teaching for understanding
Views of the same and different in mathematical reasoning	Reasoning from data
	Reducing misconceptions
	Developing ideas and theories
	The nature of science
	Understanding text genres

FIGURE 5.1. Comprehension-related topics in mathematics and science education research.

might be with narrative text and general informational materials, it does not attend to the particulars of analyzing a mathematical task or problem, comparing a mathematical problem to other problems already encountered, selecting and evaluating a strategy appropriate to learning in a mathematical context, or engaging in sense making from a problem-and-solution perspective.

In science, researchers are interested in ways that students activate prior knowledge around specific science concepts and issues. In one study, researchers explored the influence of prior knowledge activation on the comprehension of graphical information (Wu & Krajcik, 2006). The context for the study was graphical information depicting various measures of water quality. Teachers guided students to design investigations, provided guidelines for data analysis, and modeled the use of inscriptions to answer important questions. Eventually, students learned how to analyze data and use inscriptions to support their inquiry but only when they connected their work with the data to the purposes of interacting with the data and their own experiences with water quality in their community.

From a literacy research standpoint, recommending prior knowledge activation has been a long-standing, evidence-based tradition (Pressley & Hilden, 2006). However, this recommendation is often made in general terms and without attention to the specific ways that prior knowledge may need to be pressed into action to understand, for example, graphical data. The irony exists that while well-intentioned literacy researchers foist generic teaching activities on content-area teachers, their efforts are often rebuffed because those general activities do not bear specific enough relationships to the disciplinary problems at hand.

ADOLESCENTS AND STRATEGIES FOR LEARNING IN TECHNOLOGICAL ENVIRONMENTS

The literature review of adolescents and strategies for learning in technological environments epitomizes our concern about the credibility of research-based evidence. In this review, we used the same process as in the other reviews. We looked through ERIC and PsychInfo using search chains that drew on combinations of the following descriptors: "content-area reading," "content-area writing," "middle school students," "high school students," "reading," "writing," "literacy," "computer," "tech," and "Internet." We carefully examined print or online versions of eight specific journals: the *American Journal of Distance Education*, *Distance Education*, the *Journal of Adolescent and Adult Literacy*, the *Journal of Literacy Research*, the *Journal of Research on Technology in Education*, *Reading Research and Instruction*, *Reading Research Quarterly*, and *Technology and Learning*. On the recommendation of an expert in the field, we also used Google Scholar (*scholar.google.com*) to identify potential journals and articles for consideration. Through this process, we identified 31 articles for further consideration. However, when we applied our inclusion criteria— articles should be subjected to peer review, be conducted in intact class groups, include study participants from U.S. students in grades six through 12, have incorporated a pre- and postdesign to measure intervention or strategy effectiveness, and be published between 2000 and 2006—the collection of articles was decimated. While discouraging, what became clear from this effort were the conclusions that when technology-focused research articles are published, the articles tend to examine the out-of-school literacies of students. When classrooms contexts are explored, the technologies themselves, not the students' literacy practices, tend to become the primary subject matter.

With the shift from a historically strategies-oriented, "content-area literacy" moniker (cf. Alvermann & Moore, 1991; Moore, Readence, & Rickelman, 1983) to a more student-focused label of "adolescent literacy" (Moore, Bean, Birdyshaw, & Rycik, 1999), researchers have begun to emphasize students and their out-of-school literacies (Moje, 2002; Moje, Dillon, & O'Brien, 2000). For example, in recent years, researchers have detailed the literacy practices of adolescents and chat rooms (cf. Albright, Purohit, & Walsh, 2002; Morgan & Beaumont, 2003), instant messaging (Lewis & Fabos, 2005), rap and hip-hop music (cf. Paul, 2000), and television (cf. Fisherkeller, 2000). Some researchers have tried to understand how gender impacts technological literacy practices (cf. Chandler-Olcott & Mahar, 2003; Guzzetti & Gamboa, 2004; Kadijevich, 2000; Miller, Schweingruber, & Brandenburg, 2001).

Not all research on adolescent literacy captures practices outside the classroom. However, it seems that when researchers do focus on technology use inside the classroom, the questions of interest are often what Papert (1987) labeled as "technocentric" in nature. Papert uses this term to refer to the "tendency to think of 'computers' . . . as agents that act directly on thinking and learning; they betray what are really the most important components of educational situations—people and cultures" (p. 23). Our examination of the literature base suggests that research of this type is prevalent. For example, several recent articles sought to determine whether a particular technology had a significant effect on improving desirable outcomes (e.g., Martindale, Pearson, Curda, & Pilcher, 2003) rather than describing the diverse interactions of adolescents with the technology. Technocentric research questions are indeed important, but they must not be the only kind.

An important step in deepening our understanding of strategies for adolescent learning in technological environments is to focus on student–technology interactions inside classrooms. The research we need must help us understand at the student level what actual adolescent technological literacy practices are involved when significant academic learning outcomes are measured. We need research that captures the comprehension strategies school-successful students use as well as the strategies used by students who are less successful by traditional school measures. These nuanced depictions will help us better understand the richness and diversity with which adolescents interact with the content, pedagogies, and technologies of the classroom.

THE RESEARCH WE NEED

From the four reviews, several conclusions can be drawn about the current state of research on strategies available for improving adolescents' learning from texts. First, there is an astonishing scarcity of research. Not only is the research rare, but any research that exists tends to be short in duration and narrowly defined. While there are some promising interventions, particularly for struggling adolescent readers and writers, the research is not yet clear about whether these interventions will reduce gaps between underperforming and achieving students. Especially problematic is the lack of understanding for how generic learning strategies generated by literacy researchers connect to the particulars of learning problems and opportunities in the content areas. Finally, adolescents' experiences with technology are growing faster than the insights generated by researchers and curriculum theorists. It is clear that, despite the authoritative reports and policy proclamations, a great deal of research still needs be done with regard to improving adolescents' cognitive strategies with texts. We suggest research in at least three areas:

1. *Research on how literacy knowledge and skill supports or hinders adolescents within content-area contexts.* Considerable effort has been expended within the past 50 years to illuminate the literacy demands and opportunities for young children in the first 3 years of school. More recently, equally expansive efforts have been directed toward the literacy development of preschool children. The same claim cannot be made for students in the upper elementary grades or for adolescents. As a result, little is known about patterns of achievement or failure in the upper grades, and particularly within and across the content areas. The dearth of information about literacy in these educational contexts has several major repercussions.

First, there is little understanding of the development of learning strategies with texts as students progress into more sophisticated texts and disciplinary contexts. Thus, despite raised expectations in the form of curriculum standards and testing, there is no sense of the norm for what students could or should be able to know and do as they progress through the upper grades. This raises questions too about the standards themselves and their appropriateness at different ages and grade levels. We need more research about the development of literacy knowledge and skill, particularly with strategies for learning from content-area texts.

A related issue concerns how to help struggling readers. Without a model of development or a sense of reasonable expectations, the only way we currently have for identifying struggling readers consists of classroom and state tests. However, what if the standards reflected in those assessments are wrong? What if a "normal" pattern of development consists of struggle as well as success? Even more troubling is the fact that this lack of insight into what is appropriate makes it difficult to assess which interventions might actually "work" for struggling readers. Will interventions that help students perform tasks and gain knowledge from texts in the here and now translate into, for example, successful school-to-work transitions? There is a need for research that further problematizes the notion of struggling readers while expanding ideas about interventions for the here and now, in classrooms, and strategies that might contribute to lifelong learning.

2. *Research on how to help teachers understand the interplay of literacy and disciplinary purposes, tools, models, and understandings.* It is important to recall that teachers are at the nexus of many of the issues discussed here. Teachers are responsible for whole-class interventions that help students acquire strategies for learning from texts. Teachers guide struggling readers. Teachers are rarely generic but are disciplinary in their focus. And teachers, with appropriate supports, are in an excellent position to close the technology gap between home and school.

Unfortunately, the research that would provide pragmatic tools for these instructional roles has been few and far between. While there exists a plethora of teaching activities that have been enshrined in the methods textbooks devoted to content-area literacy, very few of these activities have been connected through research to promoting strategies for independent learning from texts. These generic activities will lead students to identify topics and concepts, but they do little to empower students to comprehend texts on their own (Conley, in press). Research needs to evaluate these activities as well as others that have been proven to work in elementary classrooms with regard to their efficacy for promoting students' knowledge of how to learn from texts.

However, this research will fall short if it is not accompanied by concerns for disciplinary texts and concepts. Researchers need to reverse the pattern of recommending generic learning strategies for complex disciplinary contexts, assuming instead that the starting point for such research is the disciplinary contexts themselves. Only by examining the discipline-specific ways that learning problems and opportunities are characterized will literacy researchers be able to research strategies for learning from text with any kind of credibility. The result, if successful, could be a series of discipline-specific cases where particular kinds of problems or opportunities are worked out with the assistance of appropriate literacy strategies for learning from texts. Further research could not only provide these cases but finally and authentically define what is meant by "content-area literacy for adolescents."

3. *Research on how to help adolescents become more literate both generally and in subject-specific ways.* With a clearer picture of adolescent literacy and connections to disciplinary contexts and how teachers can help finally comes the concern for how to improve adolescent knowledge and performance. A great deal of effort has been expended by adolescent literacy researchers in the past decade to understand adolescent literacy. We now know a great deal more about the special time called "adolescence"; the development of adolescent identity; the influence of peer, family and community relationships; and the effects of gender, peer, ethnic, racial, and sexual affiliations on adolescent development. We still need to know a great deal more about how to take adolescents for who they are and help them on their journeys to who they will be. As others in this book attest, it is not enough merely to acknowledge that adolescents are special in their own right. They also deserve guidance in becoming more literate both generally and in subject-specific ways.

Research in this area is never easy. It encompasses adolescent performance in content-area classrooms, at home, in the community, and in the workplace. It means confronting statistics that announce how astonishingly large numbers of adolescents drop out of college in their freshman year despite current national efforts to increase college enrollment. It means confronting the aimlessness of the adolescents who make it through high school only to wander through their late teens and early 20s, uncertain about what they want to do with their lives. With this uncertainty often comes an inability for adolescents to understand how to prepare themselves for a possible future (Schneider & Stevenson, 2000).

Either through lines of research, longitudinal studies, or comprehensive reviews, we need to devise a much more comprehensive vision for what it means for adolescents to become literate both generally and in specific ways. Armed with this vision, adults, including teachers, parents, administrators, teacher educators, and policymakers, can all be on the same page with regard to what it means to acquire and use strategies for learning from texts. Far too often, the research as well as the recommendations have focused on the minutia of some texts and some tasks. Future research needs to take into account that the literacy strategies students learn for the here and now of classrooms and state tests must develop into literacy that lasts a lifetime. Responding to this call takes a far broader research vision than the one that has guided research on strategy instruction and learning from texts in what the current research has had to offer.

REFERENCES

Albright, J., Purohit, K., & Walsh, C. (2002). Louise Rosenblatt seeks QtAznBoi@aol.com for LTR: Using chat rooms in interdisciplinary middle school classrooms. *Journal of Adolescent and Adult Literacy, 45*(8), 692–700.

Alvermann, D., Hinchman, K., Moore, D., Phelps, S., & Waff, D. (Eds.). (2006). *Reconceptualizing the literacies in adolescents' lives.* Mahwah, NJ: Erlbaum.

Alvermann, D., & Moore, D. (1991). Secondary school reading. In R. Barr, M. Kamil, P. Mosenthal, & P. D. Pearson (Eds.), *Handbook of reading research* (Vol. 2, pp. 951–983). New York: Longman.

Berman, I., & Biancarosa, G. (2005). *Reading to achieve: A governor's guide to adolescent literacy.* Washington, DC: National Governors Association.

Biancarosa, G., & Snow, C. (2004). *Reading next—A vision for action and research in middle and high school literacy: A report from Carnegie Corporation of New York.* Washington, DC: Alliance for Excellent Education.

Bulgren, J., Deshler, D., & Lenz, B. (2007). Engaging adolescents with LD in higher order thinking about history concepts using integrated content enhancement routines. *Journal of Learning Disabilities, 40*(2), 121–133.

Calhoon, M. (2005). Effects of a peer-mediated phonological skill and reading comprehension program on reading skill acquisition for middle school students with reading disabilities. *Journal of Learning Disabilities 38*(5), 424–433.

Chandler-Olcott, K., & Mahar, D. (2003). "Tech-savviness" meets multiliteracies: Exploring adolescent girls' technology-mediated literacy practices. *Reading Research Quarterly 38*(3), 356–385.

Conley, M. (in press). Improving adolescent comprehension: Developing comprehension strategies in the content areas. In S. Israel & G. Duffy (Eds.), *Handbook of research on reading comprehension.* New York: Erlbaum.

Deshler, D., Schumaker, B., Lenz, B. K., Bulgren, J., Hock, M. F., Knight, J., et al. (2001). Ensuring content-area learning by secondary students with learning disabilities. *Learning Disabilities Research and Practice 16*(2), 96–108.

Fisherkeller, J. (2000). Everyday learning about identities among young adolescents in television culture. *Anthropology and Education Quarterly, 28,* 467–492.

Graham, S., & Perin, D. (2007). *Writing next: Effective strategies to improve writing of adolescents in middle and high schools.* Washington, DC: Alliance for Excellent Education.

Guzzetti, B. J., & Gamboa, M. (2004). Zines for social justice: Adolescent girls writing on their own. *Reading Research Quarterly, 39*(4), 408–437.

Kadijevich, D. (2000). Gender differences in computer attitude among ninth-grade students. *Journal of Educational Computing Research, 22*(2), 145–154.

Kramarski, B., Mevarech, A., & Arami, M. (2002). The effects of metacognitive instruction on solving mathematically authentic tasks. *Education Studies in Mathematics, 49*, 225–250.

Lewis, C., & Fabos, B. (2005). Instant messaging, literacies, and social identities. *Reading Research Quarterly, 40*(4), 470–501.

Manset-Williams, G., & Nelson, J. (2005). Balanced, strategic reading instruction for upper elementary and middle school students with reading disabilities: A comparative study of two approaches. *Learning Disabilities Quarterly, 28*, 59–74.

Martindale, T., Pearson, C., Curda, L., & Pilcher, J. (2003). Effects of online instructional application on reading and mathematics standardized test scores. *Journal of Research on Technology in Education, 37*(4), 349–360.

Mastropiere, M., Scruggs, T., Mohler, L., Beranak, M., Spencer, V., Boone, R. T., et al. (2001). Can middle school students with serious reading difficulties help each other and learn anything? *Learning Disabilities Research and Practice, 16*(1), 18–27.

Miller, L. M., Schweingruber, H., & Brandenburg, C. L. (2001). Middle school students' technology practices and preferences: Re-examining gender differences. *Journal of Educational Multimedia and Hypermedia, 10*(2), 125–140.

Moje, E. B. (2002). Re-framing adolescent literacy research for new times: Studying youth as a resource. *Reading Research and Instruction, 41*, 207–224.

Moje, E. B., Dillon, D. R., & O'Brien, D. G. (2000). Re-examining the roles of the learner, the text, and the context in secondary literacy. *Journal of Educational Research, 93*, 165–180.

Moore, D., Alvermann, D., & Hinchman, K. A. (Eds.). (2000). *Struggling adolescent readers.* Newark, DE: International Reading Association.

Moore, D. W., Bean, T. W., Birdyshaw, D., & Rycik, J. A. (1999). *Adolescent literacy: A position statement.* Newark, DE: International Reading Association.

Moore, D. W., Readence, J. E., & Rickelman, R. (1983). An historical exploration of content area reading instruction. *Reading Research Quarterly, 28*(4), 419–438.

Morgan, W., & Beaumont, G. (2003). A dialogic approach to argumentation: Using a chat room to develop early adolescent students' argumentative writing. *Journal of Adolescent and Adult Literacy, 47*(2), 146–157.

National Association of Secondary School Principals. (2005). *Creating a culture of literacy: A guide for middle and high school principals.* Reston, VA: Author.

National Association of State Boards of Education. (2005). *Reading at risk: The state response to the crisis in adolescent literacy.* Alexandria, VA: Author.

National Reading Panel. (2000). *Report of the National Reading Panel: An evidence-based assessment of the scientific research literature on reading and its implications for reading instruction.* Washington, DC: National Institutes of Health, National Institute of Child Health and Human Development.

Papert, S. (1987). Computer criticism versus technocentric thinking. *Educational Researcher, 16*(1), 22–30.

Paul, D. (2000). Rap and orality: Critical media literacy, pedagogy, and cultural synchronization. *Journal of Adolescent and Adult Literacy, 44*(3), 246–251.

Pressley, M., & Hilden, K. (2006). Cognitive strategies: Production deficiencies and successful strategy instruction everywhere. In W. Damon, R. M. Lerner, D. Kuhn, & R. S. Siegler (Eds.), *Handbook of child psychology: Vol. 2. Cognition, perception, and language* (pp. 511–556). Hoboken, NJ: Wiley.

Raphael, T., & Pearson, P. (1985). Increasing student awareness of sources of information for answering questions. *American Educational Research Journal, 22,* 217–237.

Schneider, B., & Stevenson, D. (2000). *The ambitious generation: America's teenagers, motivated but directionless.* New Haven, CT: Yale University Press.

Snow, C., & Biancarosa, G. (2003). *Adolescent literacy and the achievement gap: What do we know and where do we go from here?* New York: Carnegie Corporation.

Snow, C. E., Burns, M. S., & Griffin, P. (Eds.). (1998). *Preventing reading difficulties in young children.* Washington, DC: National Academy Press.

U.S. Department of Education. (2007, March 29). Striving Readers Program homepage. Retrieved from *www.ed.gov/programs/strivingreaders/index.html*

Valleley, R., & Shriver, M. (2003). An examination of the effects of repeated readings with secondary students. *Journal of Behavioral Education, 12*(1), 55–76.

Wu, H., & Krajcik, J. (2006). Inscriptional practices in two inquiry-based classrooms: A case study of seventh graders' use of data tables and graphs. *Journal of Research in Science Teaching, 43*(1), 63–95.

6

What Is Mathematical Literacy?

Exploring the Relationship between Content-Area Literacy and Content Learning in Middle and High School Mathematics

JON R. STAR
SHARON STRICKLAND
AMANDA HAWKINS

Not long ago, we (a group of former middle and high school mathematics teachers and now mathematics education researchers and secondary mathematics teacher educators) participated in a series of conversations with literacy researchers about content-area literacy. This phrase, "content-area literacy," was not one that we used regularly or heard our mathematics education colleagues use, and as a result we were not sure what it meant. Our literacy colleagues, in contrast, seemed quite comfortable speaking about content-area literacy. And to our surprise, our literacy colleagues (who had very limited background in mathematics or mathematics education) seemed to know much more about content-area literacy in *mathematics* than we did.

As a result of these conversations, we decided to investigate the construct of content-area literacy in mathematics. We initially assumed that being literate in a content area such as mathematics was tightly linked to the nature of the content area. So content-area literacy in mathematics would be quite different from content-area literacy in science, given that science and mathematics are two very different disciplines (in terms both of domains of knowledge and epistemologies). In other words, we began by thinking of content-area literacy as *content-area* literacy, with the emphasis on the content area in which one was developing literacy. Thus, content-area literacy in mathematics would be centrally concerned with what it means to be literate in mathematics.

We soon realized that our initial assumption was at odds with the ways that many literacy educators thought about content-area literacy. It appeared that many viewed this construct as content-area *literacy*, with the emphasis on literacy. This alternative conception of content-area *literacy* appeared to focus on domain-general literacy (e.g., reading and writing skills) but using examples from a particular content area and using the class time allocated to that content area. For example, content-area *literacy* in mathematics might involve an emphasis on developing students' reading and writing skills by reading mathematics texts or writing papers in mathematics classes. We found further support for this view of content-area *literacy* in various texts for preservice teachers that accompany literacy courses (Alvermann & Phelps, 2002; Readence, Bean, & Baldwin, 2001; Vacca & Vacca, 2004). Many of these texts use the phrase *"content-area literacy"* in their titles and their chapters discuss the kinds of activities that can be done in content classes such as mathematics, science, history, and so on, that can promote the development of reading and writing skills.

This chapter is a result of our reflections on these two quite different views of content-area literacy. We begin by critically examining the second perspective, content-area *literacy*, as we find this view problematic from our perspective as middle and secondary mathematics educators. We then discuss the former perspective, *content-area* literacy in mathematics (which mathematics educators appear to call "mathematical literacy").

We again note that we are literacy outsiders; we do not claim to have deep knowledge about literacy or content-area *literacy*. But given our status as literacy *outsiders* but content *insiders* (particularly at the middle and secondary school level), we feel that our reflections have the potential to be useful to those in the field of literacy who may not be as grounded in a particular content area such as mathematics.

CRITICALLY EXAMINING CONTENT-AREA *LITERACY*

According to our literacy colleagues and the preservice teacher texts that we consulted, content-area *literacy* refers to reading and writing activities that are embedded within content courses. With respect to mathematics classes, this might mean that students may or should engage in activities that involve and strengthen reading and writing skills.

What sorts of activities might a middle and high school mathematics teacher use to strengthen students' reading and writing? We generated a long list that we have used or that some of our colleagues have used, including keeping a mathematics journal, reading newspaper articles related to mathematics, reading the mathematics textbook or other mathematics-related books, writing research papers on topics in mathematics, and writing paragraph explanations to accompany solutions to mathematics problems. Each of these activities has the potential to help students become better readers and writers, which we agree is one important goal of middle and secondary school education.

However, we see two serious problems with the use of these content-area *literacy* activities in mathematics. First, in the ways that they are typically implemented, each of these activities has great potential to be devoid of content learning. In other words, while these activities may help students learn to read and write (and may also help motivate students by situating mathematics in the real world, communicate their ideas about mathematics, or even help students to learn more about the history of mathematics—all of which are very important learning goals), it is not clear whether or how these activities help students learn mathematics. What mathematics do students learn from keeping a mathematics journal or from writing a mathematics history paper? Do these activities help students learn the mathematics that they might see on a unit test or a standardized test, for example? Based on our experience, content-area *literacy* activities implemented in mathematics class typically do not help students learn mathematics.

A second serious problem with content-area *literacy* activities in mathematics is that they may not help students enhance their reading and writing skills. As an example, consider the seemingly simple content-area *literacy* recommendation that students should be encouraged to read their mathematics book. The assumption behind this recommendation is that students' ability to read nonmathematics books can be potentially enhanced by reading mathematics texts in mathematics class. We find this assumption to be rather naive and believe that it reflects quite limited knowledge about mathematics and mathematics texts. The narrative structure in mathematics texts is quite different from that in other texts. Many mathematics books have few, if any, paragraphs of text, but rather are composed of a series of worked examples with sentences sprinkled in here and there. The "reader" is supposed to look sequentially at the worked examples, read whatever accompanying text might be present, and attempt to understand the procedures or concepts as illustrated in the worked examples. Understanding or comprehension is assessed by attempting problems, while referring back to the worked examples when necessary. Arguably, many mathematics texts are not written to be read as one would read a more narrative book. If mathematics teachers were to implement this content-area *literacy* task and assign students to "read" their mathematics book (in the way that mathematics educators think that a mathematics book should be read), it is not clear whether this kind of "reading" would have any impact on how students read other nonmathematics books. So this raises the question about whether reading a mathematics text is desirable from a content-area *literacy* perspective at all.

Despite these concerns, it is certainly the case that very talented teachers might be able to ensure that literacy-building activities support *both* literacy and mathematics learning; perhaps this synthesis of literacy and content learning is what we should hope and expect teachers should be able to do when focusing on content-area *literacy*. But our experiences as teachers suggest that this kind of integration is extremely difficult. Most teachers who do literacy-building (or content-area *literacy*) activities in mathematics classes find that such activities do *not* serve their mathematics content learning goals and vice versa. As a result, many teachers feel that they have to make a difficult choice: to focus either on mathematics learning goals or on literacy goals.

Complicating this perceived choice between mathematics and literacy learning goals, many mathematics teachers do not feel qualified to teach reading and writing. Most colleges and universities require minimal coursework to ensure that graduates (e.g., mathematics majors) emerge with sufficient literacy skills, regardless of students' majors. Yet, even if a mathematics teacher has the ability to read and write quite well, he or she may not have the necessary skills to teach others how to read and write well. Certainly middle and secondary mathematics teacher preparation courses do not prepare preservice mathematics teachers to teach reading and writing. So while mathematics teachers can implement content-area *literacy* tasks, many teachers do not have great confidence in their ability to use these tasks to help students learn to read and write. Yet schools and districts often require mathematics teachers to include some content-area *literacy* activities, which might lead some mathematics teachers to use these tasks sparingly, superficially, and even begrudgingly.

In sum, our initial attempts to understand what content-area *literacy* means in middle and secondary mathematics classrooms indicates that many content-area *literacy* activities focus on literacy goals and not (and perhaps at the expense of) mathematics learning goals. As a result, mathematics teachers may feel that they are not qualified to teach literacy and/or that the literacy activities can only be done at the expense of students' mathematics learning.

CONTENT-AREA NUMERACY: A THOUGHT EXPERIMENT

We imagine that some literacy researchers might agree that the goals of content-area *literacy* activities are primarily about literacy and deliberately not about mathematics learning. Despite the challenges of implementing these activities while also addressing mathematical learning goals, some might continue to strongly recommend that such literacy activities should be in mathematics classrooms. We are concerned that such a recommendation may not appreciate the challenges faced by mathematics teachers who attempt to implement content-area *literacy* activities. As a way to make our concerns more concrete, we propose the following thought experiment.

Imagine that a new districtwide policy mandates that teachers in all middle and high school subject areas implement content-area *numeracy* activities in their classrooms. Content-area *numeracy* activities are aimed at improving students' ability to use mathematics in everyday life. Given U.S. students' mediocre scores on standardized mathematics exams and the importance of mathematics to students' later course taking and career choices, it has been determined that students need to see and do mathematics in all of their subject areas—not just in mathematics class.

A committee of mathematics teachers has generated a list of content-area *numeracy* tasks that can improve students' numeracy skills in each subject area. For example, it is recommended that English teachers have their students count the number of words on consecutive pages of a text and then find the sum, difference, product, and quotient of these word counts using several standard and alternative algorithms. English teachers are also urged to take a vocabulary word, create a code by assigning a number to each letter of the word, "spell" words in numbers rather than letters, and then do various code-breaking activities. In U.S. history, teachers are encouraged to take the year of an important event (e.g., 1776), reverse the digits (e.g., 6771), subtract the two numbers, and then discuss what, if any, patterns exist when this procedure is implemented with different dates. History teachers should also work with their students to find the spherical equations for the arcs that connect two world capitals such as London and Ankara.

How might English and U.S. history teachers react to these recommendations or to this thought experiment more generally? We can imagine several kinds of reactions. First, teachers in nonmathematics subject areas might feel that content-area *numeracy* activities have little or nothing to do with learning in their particular content area. Counting words on pages of a text and finding sums and products does not help students address English course goals; looking for number patterns in dates of important events does not help U.S. history students learn U.S. history course content.

Second, nonmathematics teachers might question whether they are qualified to facilitate these content-area *numeracy* activities. Many nonmathematics teachers in middle and secondary school had very little required mathematics as part of their college majors and received no training in how to teach mathematics as part of their teacher training. While nonmathematics teachers could implement these content-area *numeracy* activities if they were required to, many would not be comfortable doing so, as the activities typically involve mathematics that is beyond the skill set of anyone but mathematics teachers.

Third, nonmathematics teachers might feel that the people who designed and recommended these content-area *numeracy* tasks do not know much about other content areas—they just know mathematics. For example, a U.S. history teacher might argue that the content-area *numeracy* task using dates and reversed digits is based on an assumption that learning history is largely about memorizing dates. But, arguably, newer methods of teaching history rely less on dates and more on understanding historical and cultural processes and events, which raises questions about the appropriateness of this content-area *numeracy* task.

All three of these critiques are quite valid. Our purpose in discussing this thought experiment is to claim that these critiques about content-area *numeracy* are parallel to some of our concerns about content-area *literacy*. First, content-area *literacy* activities typically do not have to do with learning mathematics, except in exceptional circumstances with an outstanding teacher. Second, we as mathematics teachers do not feel particularly qualified to conduct activities that focus primarily on reading and writing—this is not part of our training. And third, we feel that the content-area *literacy* tasks that we are familiar with have not generally been created by people who have deep knowledge of mathematics teaching and learning goals.

WHAT IS *CONTENT-AREA* LITERACY (OR *MATHEMATICAL* LITERACY)?

Our concerns with content-area *literacy* in mathematics led us to learn more about the alternative conception of *content-area* literacy—one that focuses on what it means to be literate in a content area. We came across the term "*mathematical* literacy" in mathematics education writings and wondered whether *mathematical* literacy was an appropriate term for *content-area* literacy. To investigate this, we performed an ERIC search for *mathematical* literacy to identify published journal articles in the past 25 years that use this specific phrase. Our search yielded 24 journal articles. We read these articles and attempted to organize what *mathematical* literacy meant to these authors.

Our analysis indicated that *mathematical* literacy can hold several different but interrelated meanings. First, about three-quarters of the articles indicated or implied that *mathematical* literacy is synonymous with mathematical *understanding*, including knowledge of content and the ability to approach mathematical problems (such as those seen in mathematics texts) logically, analytically, and thoughtfully. Second, about half of the articles indicated that mathematical literacy included an *appreciation* of mathematics, including the ability to recognize when and how mathematics is used in the real world. For example, being mathematically literate could include noticing how mathematics is used in stores, restaurants, and newspapers. Third, about one-third of the articles suggested that mathematical literacy involves the *application* of mathematics to real-world problems, including calculating tips in restaurants, working with budgets, and reading graphs in newspapers. Fourth, about one-fourth of the uses of mathematical literacy were related to the ability to *reason* mathematically, including mathematical communication.

Not surprisingly, authors' use of mathematical literacy maps well to the various incarnations of the mathematics learning goals put forward by the National Council of Teachers of Mathematics (NCTM), including standards documents from 1989 to the present (NCTM, 1989, 2000). However, and interestingly, stereotypical literacy activities such as reading, writing, reasoning, and communicating were clearly secondary and supporting components of mathematical literacy to mathematics educators, with content understanding playing a much larger and more significant role.

Our reading of mathematics educators' perceptions of *content-area* (*mathematical*) literacy underscores our earlier point that (from the perspective of mathematics educators) content-area *literacy* appears to be quite different from *content-area* literacy. The former appears to be largely about reading and writing, while the latter is largely about mathematical understanding. Stated somewhat differently, content-area *literacy* can be faulted for its disconnection with content, while *content-area* (*mathematical*) literacy is perhaps guilty of an insufficient connection to literacy.

MOVING FORWARD

This chapter represents our initial exploration into content-area literacy and our attempt to articulate problems with (what we perceive to be) a common conception of content-area literacy. We see several interesting avenues for continued thinking in this area.

A first step forward would be for us to become more educated about what we have referred to as content-area *literacy*. It may be the case that we are mischaracterizing or misunderstanding how literacy researchers use and operationalize this phrase, even though we are confident that we accurately convey what many in the mathematics education community understand about content-area *literacy*. If so, perhaps some of our qualms about content-area *literacy* need reexamining.

Regardless, however, we feel that content-area literacy can become much more grounded in content. The distinction between content-area *literacy* and *content-area* literacy seems unnecessary. Perhaps it is possible to reconceptualize content-area literacy to create more balance? Doing so would require much greater coordination and communication between the literacy educators and the mathematics educators, particularly at the middle and secondary school levels. But such a reconceptualization would have many potential benefits. In particular, mathematics teachers might be more willing to work on (and feel more capable of improving) students' reading and writing if content-area literacy activities were designed to more easily integrate literacy and mathematics learning goals (which may in turn help students in both of these areas).

REFERENCES

Alvermann, D., & Phelps, J. (2002). *Content reading and literacy: Succeeding in today's diverse classrooms.* Boston: Allyn & Bacon.

National Council of Teachers of Mathematics. (1989). *Curriculum and evaluation standards for school mathematics.* Reston, VA: Author.

National Council of Teachers of Mathematics. (2000). *Principles and standards for school mathematics.* Reston, VA: Author.

Readence, J. E., Bean, T. W., & Baldwin, R. S. (2001). *Content-area literacy: An integrated approach.* Dubuque, IA: Kendall/Hunt.

Vacca, R., & Vacca, J. (2004). *Content area reading: Literacy and learning across the curriculum.* New York: Allyn & Bacon.

7

Literacy in Science

Using Agency in the Material World
to Expand the Conversation

STEVE FORBES TUCKEY
CHARLES ANDERSON

In keeping with the theme of the book, this chapter is about adolescent literacy in the content areas. Since we are science educators, our focus is on scientific literacy. Yet what *is* "scientific literacy"? Coined in the 1950s (Conant, 1952; Hurd, 1958; McCurdy, 1958), it is a familiar term in science education scholarship and policy. For example, here is a definition from *Science for All Americans,* a basic science education policy document:

> The science-literate person is one who is aware that science, mathematics, and technology are interdependent human enterprises with strengths and limitations; understands key concepts and principles of science; is familiar with the natural world and recognizes both its diversity and unity; and uses scientific knowledge and scientific ways of thinking for individual and social purposes. (Rutherford & Ahlgren, 1990)

This definition makes sense to us, and apparently to science educators in general. However, this definition seems different from the National Reading Commission's suggestions for effective literacy instruction within the classroom:

> Adolescents respond to the literacy demands of their subject area classes when they have appropriate background knowledge and strategies for reading a variety of texts. Effective instruction develops students' abilities to comprehend, discuss, study, and write about multiple forms of text (print, visual, and oral) by taking into account what they are capable of doing as everyday users of language and literacy. (Alvermann, 2001, p. 2)

And this, in turn, seems quite different from the definition of literacy as control of secondary discourses offered by Gee, in which he defines a discourse as

> a socially accepted association among ways of using language, of thinking, and of acting that can be used to identify oneself as a member of a socially meaningful group or "social network." . . . Think of discourse as an "identity kit" which comes complete with the appropriate costume and instructions on how to act and talk so as to take a particular role that others will recognize. (1991, p. 3)

Even if we consider "science" as a modifier for the extant term "literacy," we can recognize distinct perspectives in these three quotes. Though it is often the work of scholarship to find and explore such differences, we write this text as means to further conversation and collaboration.

In order for science educators to have a productive discussion about literacy with literacy scholars like Gee and Alvermann, we need to do some work to understand one another's assumptions. Do the "social purposes" in *Science for All Americans* share similar goals with what Gee refers to as "social networks"? Are there ways in which Alvermann's "strategies" improve students' ability to master a discourse of scientific knowledge? How does interacting with the natural (or, as we will refer to it, the material[1]) world interface with texts and discourse within a classroom? These are examples of the entangled questions that are of

---

[1]We make use of the phrase "material world" since it encompasses what often is *intended* by terms like "physical," "technological," and "real," while it is less likely to provoke difficult ontological and epistemological questions about the existence of a singular "reality," irrespective of our observations of it. This brackets some issues for the purpose of allowing a discussion of other issues, and avoids the spiraling debate around questions of a singular real world in which we all live. This is not to say that such questions are unimportant—in fact, we believe that they constitute some of the gaps between the research traditions—but that they are mostly unproductive for the pragmatic purposes of teaching.

great interest to us as science educators as we try to engage in that productive discussion with other scholars. This chapter is about our attempts to sort out the tangle.

We can start with something that all the definitions above have in common. All of the authors share a concern for the enhancement of student "agency," by which they mean increasing students' ability to do things as adults of which they might not otherwise be capable. So, to pursue this line of reasoning, we may consider "literacy" as the enhancement of agency with respect to texts. In our thinking, expanding the term by adding the adjective "scientific" provides an additional dimension: scientific literacy involves agency with the world of texts and information, in connection to the material world. Even so, we are aware that agreement (whether inside or outside content areas) about terms like "literacy" is rare. Therefore, we aim to examine this term by exploring alternative interpretations of a specific teaching event that involves science and literacy. In the process, we hope to expand the larger conversation around literacy by sharing a view from within science education and suggesting future lines of research that will inform our work and that of our teacher candidates.

THE CASE OF JENNIFER AND JUAN

As science education researchers and science teacher educators, we have an interest in the role of literacy in science classrooms. As our students—preservice science teachers—come back from teaching experiences in classrooms, they raise questions about how to engage with and help students better understand the subject matter (i.e., increase scientific literacy). In order to illustrate the interplay between research and practice in a way that might inform the ongoing conversations about literacy in science, we turn to a slightly fictionalized example of such a situation.

Jennifer is an eager and dedicated student of science with a great desire to teach students. Her backgrounds in biology and chemistry are strong, as is her grasp of the interpersonal nature of teaching. She cares about helping students understand scientific concepts, and this concern is evident in the way she actively pursues alternative teaching techniques. After one particularly frustrating experience working with a student in a one-on-one setting, she came to us with the deceptively simple question, "What do I do now?" Her question, posed in an honest state of bewilderment, suggested both her frustration with a teaching situation apparently gone awry as well as her faith in *our* ability to provide an answer.

She explained the situation in the following manner:

> "I was working with Juan, my student, on the causes of seasons, and he didn't seem to understand the worksheet we were using. It asked him to read a paragraph, look at a drawing of how the Earth's tilt changes with respect to the Sun, and answer some questions. He answered the questions, but when I talked with him about it, he couldn't explain any of it."

It seemed that Jennifer was trying to make use of a particular piece of teaching material (the worksheet) for the purpose of teaching the student a broad concept (the effect of axial tilt on seasonal changes), and the student was not displaying an adequate understanding of the concept outside the context of the worksheet. It was pretty clear that "literacy" was involved; it was also quite clear that the student was not feeling like an effective agent with respect to the worksheet or the causes of seasonal change. The question sat on the table before us: What would *we* do in her position?

We believe that the authors quoted above—Rutherford and Ahlgren, Alvermann, and Gee—would answer Jennifer's question in quite different ways, so we can use the format of Jennifer's case as a means to discuss two specific things: our view of research traditions regarding science literacy and our suggestions for thought and action regarding literacy in science. By doing so, it is our sincere hope that we will find both ways to better answer Jennifer's question and directions for future research: the research we have and the research we need.

A FRAMEWORK OF TRADITIONS AND COMMONPLACES

We suggest three traditions of educational research by their respective areas of focus: *content*-oriented (illustrated by the Rutherford & Ahlgren quote above), *strategies*-oriented (illustrated by the Alvermann quote), and *discourse*-oriented (illustrated by the Gee quote). Researchers and practitioners from these traditions would have different ways of analyzing Jennifer's problem and different recommendations about what she should do.

We need some way of understanding differences in perspectives and recommendations—commonplaces for conversation. We borrow the notion of "commonplaces" from the work of Schwab (1969) and all those who added to the conversation thereafter as a means for understanding the complexities of research on literacy in science. For instance, regardless of one's perspective, a discussion about curriculum theory includes something about certain common topics (e.g., students, teachers, content, and milieu). Participants in such a conversation may not agree on the particulars of what is included in "content" or on the specific qualifications that define a "teacher." Yet organizing the discussion around these commonplaces provides easier entry into the conversation and opportunities for relevant, constructive critique. With this in mind, we provide a framework of commonplaces for a conversation around the topic of scientific literacy.

Table 7.1 shows the framework with which we make our observations about the research we have and speculate on the research we need around the issue of literacy in secondary science. We use the commonplaces (rows) to examine different research traditions (columns). These commonplaces, adapted from those suggested by Schwab and others, are the aspects of conversations about teaching science literacy that are addressed by researchers in all traditions, though with differing interpretations:

1. The kinds of "texts" that represent authoritative scientific knowledge.
2. Expectations for the role of the teacher.
3. Ideas about how students learn.
4. What it means to be scientifically literate.

Perspectives on these commonplaces differ across the research community, and so we choose to use them as a means for examining broad traditions in research. In order to further examine these research traditions, and the substance of their intersections with the commonplaces we nominate below, we suggest ways that researchers and practitioners in each tradition might address Jennifer's dilemma.

EXAMINING THE COMMONPLACES: THE RESEARCH WE HAVE

The intersections in the table broadly represent the perspectives of each research tradition with respect to commonplaces in discussions about literacy. The goal of this section is to use the case of Jennifer and Juan to compare these perspectives and the bodies of research they represent.

TABLE 7.1. Commonplaces for Considering Different Research Traditions

	Content-oriented	Strategies-oriented	Discourse-oriented
Nature of "texts:" authoritative sources of scientific knowledge	1. Data from direct experience with the material world 2. Representations of data, patterns, models	Knowledge and practices represented through language (e.g., reading, writing, speaking, listening)	Semiotic representations (including language, customs, ways of manipulating objects, etc.) of cultural models or funds of knowledge
Expectations for the role of teacher	Teacher as content expert; providing material experiences for students	Teacher as strategy expert; modeling thinking and action for making use of texts	Teacher as expert in developing opportunities for students to participate in scientific discourse
Ideas about how students learn	Experiences with material world and sense making	Strategies for interrogating and interpreting texts of particular genres	Experiences with different discourse communities and their practices
Ideas about "scientifically literate" students	Scientific knowledge and understanding developed through interaction with the material world	Scientific knowledge and understanding developed through interrogation and interpretation of texts	Scientific knowledge and understanding developed through legitimate participation in communities of practice

Content-Oriented Research

Our own perspective on science education is mostly in line with the broad body of research that is oriented toward the importance of science concepts (content) that map onto or attempt to explain experiences in the material world. That is to say that we identify closely with the content-oriented research on science education. For specific examples of this tradition in the larger community, one need look no further than the large variety of state and national science standards (cf. American Association for the Advancement of Science, 1990, 1993; Champagne, Lovitts, & Calinger, 1989; National Research Council, 1996, 2000) most of which are authored by scientists and science educators. In these documents, ample attention is paid to explanations of the material world, as well as to the processes by which scientific knowledge is generated, tested, and put to use. The work of researchers like Driver, Squires, Rushworth, and Wood-Robinson (1994) and Duit (2007) provide insight into this research tradition, in particular, a subset of content-oriented work known as "conceptual change research." This line of work, as an example of a kind of content-oriented research, proceeds on the grounds that the development of scientific understanding in students in some way mirrors the historical development of scientific theories and ideas.

For what we are referring to as "content-oriented science education researchers," scientifically literate students use observations in specific ways to support and inform how they understand, predict, and explain the material world. The role of "texts" in this process is important. In Table 7.1 we suggest two sorts of texts in this tradition that represent authoritative knowledge. Though this will be discussed more extensively later in the chapter, let us share briefly what we mean. In this research tradition, human-generated texts that tell the "story" of science (e.g., school textbooks and most content standards) are tools for representing this knowledge—what Karl Popper (1972) referred to as "World 3," our growing structure of theories and explanations about the material world—but are not objects or ends in themselves. These texts convey the experiences and data that are modeled by science, and are usually offered in classrooms as the "content" of science. Yet the very data and experiences upon which these representations are built are also "texts" of authoritative knowledge within content-oriented research—what Galileo (Crease, 2006) described as the "Book of Nature."

The scientific inquiry process, and the resulting data and patterns that students use to reason about the material world (discussed in greater detail later), constitute a central theme within the standards documents that epitomize content-oriented research (cf. American Association for the Advancement of Science, 1993; National Research Council, 1996). Terms such as "misconception" and "inquiry" regularly appear in content-oriented documents,[2] and are evidence of the importance placed on reasoning about and interacting with the material world. In this way, the content-oriented perspective on science is that of a subject driven by data gathered in the material world that is used for

---

[2]As a simple example of this, the *Journal for Research in Science Teaching*, one of the flagship journals in science education, has published nearly 50 articles containing the word "inquiry" in the title in the last 10 years.

constructing both inductive and deductive arguments (roughly, making and testing theories about the world). In brief, the outcome (scientific literacy) that content-oriented practitioners desire for students is a mastery of scientific tools and practices that have been identified, largely, by scientists.

In terms of the contextual aspects of teaching science, the content-oriented tradition holds particular perspectives on the role of the teacher and students' prior knowledge. Often translated into "highly qualified" in the standards documents that this tradition has been central in producing, content-oriented research tends to emphasize the need for teachers that are content experts (e.g., Zembal-Saul, Krajcik, & Blumenfeld, 2002). When discussions of students' prior knowledge arise in this research, the tendency is to focus on students' previous experiences (often bodily ones) with the material world and their reasoning about them (cf. Driver et al., 1994).

So how might content-oriented researchers and practitioners answer Jennifer's question? What could she do that would be helpful to Juan? Let us consider an answer in terms of the four commonplaces in Table 7.1.

1. *The kinds of "texts" that represent authoritative scientific knowledge.* While Jennifer and Juan have a worksheet, the worksheet would be the least interesting aspect of Jennifer's situation for most content-oriented researchers. They would be likely to put the worksheet aside and pull out a globe and flashlight, or to take Juan outside to look at the position of the Sun over a span of time and ask him what he has noticed about its apparent path across the sky. For these science educators, the most important "text" in this case is the material world itself. Physical models (like the globe and flashlight), graphs, tables, diagrams (perhaps the one on the worksheet), and simulations are also important "texts" because they show patterns in data from the material world and the conceptual models that scientists use to explain those patterns. If one text, such as Juan's worksheet, does not work in a given situation, then content-oriented practitioners would look for an improved representation—a different "text" that works better.

2. *Expectations for the role of the teacher.* Content-oriented practitioners would not be particularly interested in whether or how Jennifer might help Juan get the right answers for his worksheet. They would expect Jennifer to be concerned about whether Juan understands the causes of the seasons, understood to be the "content" at stake. Furthermore, they would expect Jennifer to find ways to understand how Juan

is thinking about the seasons and guide him to a deeper understanding. Since her background might not include appreciable experience with astronomy or the physics of planetary motion, content-oriented practitioners might suggest that Jennifer needs to better familiarize herself with more and different models and representations. By doing so, Jennifer, as content expert, would be more able to find and make use of better texts for helping Juan understand the causes of the seasons.

3. *Ideas about how students learn.* Content-oriented practitioners focus on students' experiences with and reasoning about the material world, so a common expectation would be for Jennifer to figure out the ways Juan has observed seasonal changes in the past so as to make use of them in instruction. The importance of inquiry in content-oriented instruction casts students' prior knowledge (including observations of and interactions with the material world) in a central role for creating and evaluating arguments from evidence. Providing Juan with a model for explaining seasonal changes that ignores his prior knowledge runs counter to a content-oriented notion of how students learn. The model that Jennifer supplies Juan needs to be a tool for explaining observations, so it may be necessary for Jennifer to help Juan practice making scientific observations and using the model as a tool for explaining them. Furthermore, in her work with Juan, Jennifer may find evidence of "misconceptions," which are understood as the application of models that are inappropriate for a specific situation (e.g., Juan claims the seasons are caused by the Earth's proximity to the Sun).

4. *What it means to be scientifically literate.* Though a written response on a test is certainly acceptable evidence of understanding, a verbal explanation, or a physical demonstration with the model, or a drawing would be equally convincing to content-oriented practitioners of Juan's scientific literacy—his understanding of the causes of the seasons. This understanding would enhance Juan's agency with respect to the material world, allowing him to *do* more things than he might otherwise be able to do. Specifically, Jennifer's teaching would allow Juan greater fluency in making observations of the material world, creating and recognizing patterns in those observations, and making use of (and perhaps reasoning toward) models that explain both. Though mastery of the explanations is an important component of content-oriented scientific literacy, so is the close relationship between these model-based explanations and reasoning that is grounded in the material world.

In summary, content-oriented researchers and practitioners focus in particular on students' agency with respect to the material world.

Worksheets and other written texts are potentially useful tools for helping students to understand scientific models or to construct arguments from evidence, but these texts are means to an end. The expertise of the teacher with scientific models and processes of inquiry allows him or her to engage students with the material world. Through this engagement students create and use models that better allow them to reason about the world.

Strategies-Oriented Research

In her article from which the quote at the beginning of this chapter was taken, Donna Alvermann reiterates many statements that exemplify the position of the National Reading Conference (NRC) on the question of literacy in the classroom. In the portion quoted, she identifies strategies for interpreting text as a necessary component for literacy instruction, which exemplifies a recurring theme in literacy research: the theme of strategies. According to the position statement developed by the International Reading Association Commission on Adolescent Literacy, "adolescents use print—and learn how to use print—in countless ways" (Moore, Bean, Birdyshaw, & Rycik, 1999). The centrality of printed text and the ways by which a reader makes meaning of text exemplify what we are referring to as the strategies-oriented research tradition.

As examples of strategies-oriented research, we look to Don Deshler and his colleagues at the Center for Research on Learning. Throughout their research (cf. Deshler, Hock, & Catts, 2006; Deshler, Schumaker, Harris, & Graham, 1999; Deshler & Tollefson, 2006; Hock, Schumaker, & Deshler, 2001) specific strategies for interrogating text are examined, and as a result they have designed practitioner materials for literacy instruction. The strategic instruction model (SIM) intervention program, which is an approach to teaching adolescents to become good readers and writers, represents a strategies orientation due to its specific focus on improving students' abilities to read and understand complex reading materials. Specifically, SIM addresses instruction in visual imagery, paraphrasing, and particular strategies to learn sentence, paragraph, and theme writing. Other researchers who represent this strategies orientation in their work (Dole, Duffy, Roehler, & Pearson, 1991; Duke, Purcell-Gates, Hall, & Tower, 2006–2007; Gaskins & Pressley, 2007; Gersten, Fuchs, Williams, & Baker, 2001; Kamil, 2003) have argued for the importance of key reading comprehension and writing strategies (e.g., generating questions, creating visual images, summarizing, drawing inferences, metacognitive strategies, and authentic experience).

Examining these common threads, we choose to refer to this group broadly as "*strategies*-oriented researchers" so as to allow for a more directed focus on their interests.

Throughout the strategies-oriented research literature runs the theme of strategies that allow the text user increased access to deeper meaning, which enables a text-based agency. In the case of science texts, that deeper meaning making allows the student the opportunity to "use the print" in richer ways. For strategies-oriented researchers, scientifically literate students decode and interpret scientific texts from which they derive their understanding of the subject matter. In order to do this, a set of strategies is required for focusing on and making sense of the text. Therefore, the outcome that a strategies-oriented researcher or practitioner desires for students in a science class is the mastery of how to read and interpret scientific texts and genres.

Similar to other traditions, particular perspectives on the role of the teacher and the ideas about students' learning are noticeable within this research tradition. For example, the teacher is often seen as the developer and conveyor of strategies for students who have the task of decoding and interpreting texts (e.g., Purcell-Gates, Duke, & Martineau, 2007). This is not to say that teachers are not expected to be content experts or that students never interact with the material world, but these are not the focus of such work, especially since this tradition tends to be content-neutral (i.e., strategies are useful with all modes of text). Students come to the classroom with prior knowledge of particular genres of text (often not of the scientific variety), and possess certain strategies for interrogating them (though, again, often not those of particular use in science). Therefore, students need to learn new strategies for decoding and interpreting the texts of a different genre than those to which they are more accustomed. This focus on texts belies the perception of "science" as primarily the body of knowledge extant in domain-specific books, journals, and other human-generated texts. That is to say, from this perspective, science is a text-driven enterprise—an observation that is most difficult for any scientist or science teacher to dismiss.

Based on this framing, how might strategies-oriented researchers and practitioners answer Jennifer's question? What suggestions for action might they have for Jennifer that would be helpful to Juan? Again, turning to the four commonplaces in Table 7.1, we can put forward an answer.

1. *The kinds of "texts" that represent authoritative scientific knowledge.* By virtue of it being a literal text, the worksheet that Jennifer and

Juan have to work with would be a focal point for strategies-oriented practitioners. The worksheet, with its diagrams and brief explanation, represents the authoritative scientific knowledge in this case, and therefore it is this text that requires interrogation and decoding by Juan in order for him to understand the material. As a result, strategies-oriented practitioners would propose Jennifer make use of appropriate reading comprehension strategies (e.g., activating prior knowledge, predicting, questioning, summarizing) in the service of Juan's improved understanding of the worksheet text. Other textbooks and the alternative renditions they may provide are reasonable sources for additional texts that Jennifer can use toward this end.

2. *Expectations for the role of the teacher.* In the face of concern over Juan's ability to understand the science from the worksheet and demonstrate this understanding by answering the questions, strategies-oriented practitioners consider Jennifer's role to be that of strategies expert. They expect her to model those meaning-making strategies that Juan would benefit from using in this situation. By helping Juan activate his prior knowledge, or by working with him to summarize the text he reads, Jennifer provides a strong model for how scientific texts are interpreted and used. Modeling such strategies is the desired instructional aim. Strategies-oriented practitioners expect that Jennifer will help Juan understand the relationship between the terminologies and representations that are specific to this concept. Yet capitalizing on the literacy event is about more than just this particular worksheet. By modeling such strategies, Jennifer, as strategies expert, can prepare Juan for similar future encounters with the genre while also helping him understand the cause of seasonal changes.

3. *Ideas about how students learn.* The bulk of strategies-oriented research focuses on the ways in which learners make sense of text, so such a practitioner would question Jennifer about the way Juan interacted with the worksheet. From this perspective, it is reasonable to interpret Juan's lack of understanding (the source of Jennifer's frustration) as his inability to interrogate the text. Though he may (and likely does) have many strategies for reading and interpreting texts of different genres, he may either not associate these strategies with scientific texts or those strategies may be insufficient for doing so in a meaningful way. Therefore, helping Juan to see how this particular genre is similar to and different from more familiar kinds of texts is an important goal for a strategies-oriented practitioner. Moreover, such a practitioner would pay close attention to the relationship between the language of the worksheet and the student's ability to decode and comprehend that

language—a common roadblock to learning science. As a result, a strategies-oriented practitioner would suggest that Jennifer assess and pay close attention to Juan's reading comprehension level and vocabulary so as to better match instruction with the learner's needs.

4. *What it means to be scientifically literate.* The emphasis on texts in the strategies orientation suggests that a scientifically literate student is one who has mastered the language of science. In this case, Jennifer needs to help Juan to develop and use specific strategies that will allow him to read and interpret the domain-specific language of science. Through this practice, Juan will develop agency with a wider range of texts and increase his ability to make sense of scientific explanations such as that for seasonal changes. This agency with texts will foster greater knowledge and understanding of science for Juan, allowing him to be increasingly scientifically literate.

In summary, strategies-oriented researchers and practitioners focus in particular on students' agency with respect to genres of texts. Text-books, worksheets, and other written texts are the primary sources of authoritative scientific knowledge, and the development of strategies for interpreting and understanding them is the aim of instruction. These strategies are useful tools for helping students to understand scientific content, and the teacher is the model for their implementation. Through implementing and developing these strategies for interrogating texts, students derive deeper knowledge and understanding of science and an increased fluency with multiple genres of scientific texts.

Discourse-Oriented Research

The Gee quote at the beginning of this chapter provides an example of what we refer to as "discourse-oriented research on literacy." Basing his work on the particular ways people communicate within social settings (e.g., classrooms), he reminds us that literacy needs to be considered within "the different sorts of social practices in which it is embedded" (2004, p. 14). This implies a consideration of more than reading and writing; oral language, gestures, social norms, and ways of thinking and acting are ingredients of social encounters. For Gee, Discourse (upper-case) represents broad cultural suppositions, while discourse (lower-case) relates to specific linguistic practices. This bifurcation further illustrates the complexity in notions of discourse, culture, language, and literacy within this discourse-oriented research tradition. Further examples are in order.

Science educators are quite clear that "knowing and understanding the language of science is an essential component of scientific literacy" (Wellington & Osborne, 2001, p. 139), but in contrast to the content-oriented and strategies-oriented traditions, discourse-oriented research examines the ways that domain-specific language practices circulate within social (and cultural) aspects of classrooms. Researchers like Wolff-Michael Roth (e.g., 2004), Jay Lemke (e.g., 1990), James Gee (e.g., 1991), Michael Halliday (e.g., Halliday & Martin, 1993), James Martin (e.g., Martin & Veel, 1998), Robert Veel (e.g., 1997), and Charles Bazerman (e.g., 1988) have all contributed to our understanding of the way scientific communities (be they professional or classroom-based) communicate and operate. Their work exemplifies discourse-oriented research, but we are cautious to note that we use the term "discourse" only as a means for loosely connecting together several strands of work that are more focused on the social and cultural aspects of science than are the other two traditions. Just as there were with strategies-oriented research, discourse-oriented work includes many areas of interest, including argument (e.g., Duschl, 2003; Jimnez-Aleixandre, Rodriguez, & Duschl, 2000), hybrid spaces (e.g., Lee & Roth, 2003; Moje, Collazo, Carrillo, & Marx, 2001), linguistic analysis of science in the classroom (e.g., Lemke, 1990, 2001; Michaels & O'Connor, 1991; Veel, 1997), and the intersection of bodily movement and literacy (e.g., Roth, 2004). Much like the common aim of most content-oriented researchers, discourse-oriented work is frequently geared toward understanding and improving current practices in science education, but with a stronger thread of critique running throughout. Though this work is less represented than that of content-oriented science education study, a growing body of research is published with a discourse orientation.

The social and cultural aspects of discourse-oriented research on literacy imply a different approach to thinking about texts, students, and teachers. Through such study we better understand the highly specific rules and formats of scientific texts (e.g., Fang, 2004; Lemke, 1990). Texts are broadly defined within this tradition to include semiotic representations of cultural models or funds of knowledge. These may include language (spoken and written), customs, social norms, gestures, and ways of manipulating objects, all of which are representative of science and the Western European culture that it largely represents. Those texts from outside this canon (e.g., folk wisdom and mythology) are not considered authoritative scientific knowledge, though they may represent the Discourse of many within a science classroom.

As a result of this common disconnect, this tradition also examines the role of culture in teaching and learning science. Just as Moje and colleagues (2001) provide insight into connections between students and teachers of common minority background, Barton and Yang (2000) allow for a vision of science through the eyes of a nonparticipant in the culture of power. Barton and Yang manage this by providing a literature review that decisively concludes that "the culture of power is present in all domains of science and science education" (p. 876). In examining the cultural aspects of science teaching and learning, the importance of a broadly discursive notion of literacy is underscored.

With this in mind, how might discourse-oriented researchers and practitioners respond to Jennifer? How might this perspective shape suggestions for Jennifer in her work with Juan? Turning to the four commonplaces in Table 7.1 one last time, we attempt to answer.

1. *The kinds of "texts" that represent authoritative scientific knowledge.* Since Jennifer is using multiple modes of text (expository, diagrammatical, spoken language, gesture), a discourse-oriented practitioner might choose to focus on one or more for further examination. The result of this investigation would be to consider the ways in which the scientific discourse promoted by these texts differs from Juan's home discourse. Examining the language patterns in the written text of the worksheet (e.g., the number of foreign terms) or the particular frame of reference favored by the diagram (e.g., viewing the Earth–Sun system from space), a discourse-oriented practitioner may suggest providing alternatives nearer to Juan's home discourse.

2. *Expectations for the role of the teacher.* Within this tradition, the teacher is often constructed as a sort of facilitator of cultural immersion, where the task is to bring students into meaningful contact with scientific discourse from which they can learn. As a result, a discourse-oriented practitioner would suggest that Jennifer develop opportunities for Juan to participate in the scientific discourse of the activity. This might involve her making use of alternative texts that could create a hybrid space for Juan to engage in the concepts. In doing this, Jennifer helps to provide Juan with an invitation and access to a dominant discourse (science) regarding a particular concept (seasonal changes) without disregarding his home discourses, which may differ substantially from what is represented on the worksheet.

3. *Ideas about how students learn.* Since the discourse of the worksheet and Juan's home discourses may differ, a discourse-oriented practitioner looks for ways to bridge incongruence as a means of help-

ing Juan learn science. Juan's experiences with different discourse communities and their practices is seen as an asset in the science classroom—a larger group of potential hybrid spaces. Therefore, a discourse-oriented practitioner might suggest that Jennifer start with Juan's prior knowledge of seasonal change and help him connect with more scientific discursive models, recognizing that Juan's understanding of seasons is likely embedded in culturally specific observations, norms, and practices. This may mean going from a form of everyday sense making to one based on specific forms of evidence or reasoning, so Jennifer will need to consider Juan's home discourse (e.g., verbal vs. written truth claims) and important aspects of the scientific model (e.g., Earth-based vs. space-based perspectives). Discourse-oriented practitioners would also be interested in how Juan perceives his identity with respect to the communities in which he lives. Is school a place, for example, where he can expect people to help him learn or where it is clear that he is not one of the "winners?"

4. *What it means to be scientifically literate.* Not surprisingly, discourse-oriented researchers and practitioners view science as a community practice that is culturally driven and highly language-based. From a discourse-oriented perspective, scientifically literate students operate within scientific communities of practice with the appropriate tools and characteristics of those communities. Practices and purposes are the objects of study; the world is a context for specific practices in which texts are tools for specific purposes (e.g., inquiry). The desired outcome for students is legitimate participation in communities of scientific (or scientifically literate) practice, which are sites of development for scientific knowledge and understanding. Therefore, a discourse-oriented practitioner sees Jennifer as playing the crucial role of facilitator in Juan's entry into such a community. This agency with scientific discourse will foster greater knowledge and understanding of science for Juan, allowing him access to a (scientific) literacy that might be otherwise unavailable.

In summary, discourse-oriented researchers and practitioners focus in particular on students' agency with respect to scientific discourse. Worksheets and other written texts are certainly sites of contact with this discourse (authoritative scientific knowledge), but many other modes of text are considered—many of which are socially and culturally specific. Therefore, facilitating students' legitimate participation within communities in which these texts are engaged is the aim of instruction. By doing so, students are able to access and negotiate the eracy. We followed this with examples of each tradition—content-, strategies-, and discourse-oriented research—and likely responses to Jennifer's question from each, based on how we see them. Part of opening dialogue between research traditions involves understanding the ways in which each perspective might view others. To this end, and keeping in mind our backgrounds as science content-oriented researchers, we will now try to provide some examples of the concerns that occur to us as we examine the other two perspectives. We will follow this up with a more detailed examination of content-oriented notions of scientific texts and reasoning. These discussions are meant as a means for increasing understanding (ours, as well as our readers') of different research traditions.

From the content-oriented perspective, the focus on written texts (as per the strategies orientation) is problematic for two main reasons. First, adopting a vision of literacy that primarily focuses on improving the ways in which students interrogate written texts suggests placing a diminished value on interaction with the material world. Second, there is a great deal of concern over the quality of the texts—especially commercially produced curricula (Kesidou & Roseman, 2002)—that currently are in use in science classrooms. It is our hope that a search for improved literacy strategies also would involve a serious examination of the texts that are in use.

Similarly, a content-oriented researcher or practitioner would have concerns in regards to the discourse-oriented suggestions offered to Jennifer. First, much of the context upon which the differences between discourses (home and science) depend is out of the immediate control of teachers and other practitioners. Moreover, the complexity of discourse-oriented practices is such that implementation is often difficult to negotiate for well-versed scholars, let alone novice teachers. If Jennifer were to try, for example, creating a hybrid space for Juan, it is less likely that she would understand how to do this at the level of daily practice than at a broader, holistic level. Though helpful in understanding how discourse operates within specific classroom contexts, discourse-oriented research tends to be less helpful in suggesting means for fostering specific kinds of discourse in specific classroom contexts.

In light of these concerns, it is important to understand the motivations of a content-oriented researcher or practitioner a bit better. The importance placed on experience in the material world in content-oriented science education tends to have two main consequences. First, there is less of a focus on human-generated expository texts in favor of spending more time engaged with the material world. This is not to say

tools and practices of scientific discourse, with which they develop scientific knowledge and understanding. The teacher is a facilitator for this entry into a scientific discourse community, and scientific literacy is achieved by students with control of this important secondary discourse.

Blurring and Crossing the Boundaries of Tradition

In all three of the traditions above it is our intent to use commonplaces to highlight differences in the perspectives each takes on the case of Jennifer and Juan. Regardless of which research tradition one most identifies with, the response to Jennifer's situation involves constructing a better understanding of the situation, especially of Juan as a student, and making use of that understanding as a basis for further interaction and teaching. Other chapters within this book provide excellent illustrations of how those with strategies and discourse orientations go about constructing this understanding and making use of it. In order to contribute, one of our goals is to help illustrate a content-oriented approach to understanding such a situation. Yet, before we do this, we feel it is important to note the ways in which the research traditions can and do inform each other in some productive ways.

So far in this chapter we have attempted to categorize research broadly for the purpose of examining differences in the ways the research community considers literacy. Yet our intent is not to suggest that such boundaries are fixed and nonporous. In fact, within the science education research community there is a growing concern for the treatment of literacy, as well as an understanding of how literacy research and science education research intersect. In claiming that literacy in the "fundamental sense" (i.e., reading and writing) is "central to scientific literacy," Norris and Phillips (2003) seek to open a greater dialogue between what we refer to as content- and strategies-oriented researchers. Likewise, other scholars are finding ways to bridge the gaps between these orientations and to blend notions of text, scientific reasoning, and content understanding. For example, a series of researchers have offered reading protocols that have sought to improve learning through reading (e.g., Dansereau, 1985; Palincsar, 1986; Spiegel & Barufaldi, 1994). Specifically, Spiegel and Barufaldi's (1994) work suggested that construction of graphic postorganizers would significantly improve students' recall and comprehension abilities in science.

Research on writing in science classrooms is also providing connections between content- and strategies-oriented traditions. As an example, Keys, Hand, Prain, and Collins (1999) report that students can generate meaning with evidence regarding specific scientific topics, make connections between observations and inferences, and develop metacognitive awareness about writing in science. An increasing amount of research on writing in science education has created a growing body of knowledge (e.g., Hand, Prain, Lawrence, & Yore, 1999; Holliday, Yore, & Alvermann, 1994; Keys, 1999). The focus of this research is increasingly integrating studies of written and spoken classroom text (e.g., Keys, 1997; Rivard & Straw, 2000), thus highlighting the importance of multiple modes of language use. Despite such studies addressing writing in science, the most significant concern for the bridging of content- and strategies-oriented research is in regards to issues of context. Rivard (1994) explored this issue, suggesting that decontextualized studies of writing lack "ecological validity" (p. 975). Researchers from both strategies- and content-oriented perspectives are beginning to raise similar concerns for studies of reading and speaking within science classrooms and the ways in which multiple modes of communication mix together in students' understanding of science.

In order to address such concerns, researchers are increasingly blurring the boundaries between content- and discourse-orientations with some interesting results. For example, Vellom and Anderson (1999), as a result of their study of classroom discourse around the concept of density, caution that learning science "must consist of inquiry and problem solving based on direct experience with phenomena" (p. 180), while also considering the social and cultural factors that mediate student interaction. In their work on classroom discourse, O'Connor and Michaels examine the ways in which "the literacies of home and school are not always congruent" (1993, p. 318). Similarly, Gallego and Hollingsworth suggest that personal literacies are different from school literacies, and they reflect how students "believe they should join in socially accepted discourse communities and the private ways they know they can and would like to be able to participate" (2000, p. 15).

Recognizing and examining the spaces between more disciplinary-specific literacies (e.g., science literacy) and those of students' cultures can provide fertile ground for discussion and collaboration between content-, strategies-, and discourse-oriented researchers. Such collaborations may prompt changes in each tradition that would bridge divides even more. For example, in their examination of what they call "everyday sense-making," Warren, Ballenger, Ogonowski, Rosebery, and Hudicourt-Barnes (2001) suggest that ways of knowing in other cultures may be in

conflict with those of science. Additionally, they push for the broad[ening] of science classroom discourse to include more ways of knowing that more students are able to express their conceptions. One rea[ction] of a content- or strategies-oriented researcher or practitioner migh[t] to dismiss such claims as troublesome or complicating. Yet, by allow[ing] a fuller discussion of what counts as *scientific* in the science classroo[m] and who can participate in sense making—we allow for conversat[ion] about precisely those aspects of the curriculum (e.g., inquiry, met[a] evidence-based reasoning) that we hold so dear. Moreover, class[room] conversations would allow more students to engage in the metac[ogni]tive strategies around different kinds of sense making. As a res[ult] such border crossing (or border blurring), it may be possible to [con]sider a hybrid definition of scientific literacy; scientifically literat[e stu]dents engage in communities of practice that employ strategies fo[r cre]ating and using texts that foster agency in the material world.

Just as content-oriented researchers and practitioners can le[arn a] great deal from the different perspectives, strategies- and disc[ourse]oriented researchers are already aware of science as a fertile grou[nd for] future work on literacy. Gee suggests that "all of literacy educatio[n has a] great deal to learn from scientific literacy" (2004, p. 42) in light [of the] regular multimodality of texts in science: charts, diagrams, and [equa]tions, as well as a strong presence of expository texts. Gee m[akes a] strong case for considering a broad range of texts in science class[rooms.]

> We need to devote more explicit attention to teaching students how [to] read hybrid text. We need to help them understand the conventi[ons] that connect verbal text with mathematical expressions and graphs a[nd] diagrams of all kinds. We need to help them reproduce the fusion [of] conceptual kinds and quantitative degrees that is central to scient[ific] meaning-making by giving them practice in translating back and fo[rth] among verbal accounts, mathematical expressions and calculatio[ns,] schematic diagrams, abstract graphs, and hands-on actions. (p. 4[1)]

It is this idea that motivates the next section of the chapter: [a] look at the content-oriented perspective and the potential bene[fits of ex]amining scientific texts for literacy research.

CONTENT-ORIENTED CRITIQUES AND SCIENTIFIC TEXT[S]

Our framework in Table 7.1 attempts to portray three resear[ch tradi]tions in terms of four commonplaces in discussions about scie[nce] tools and practices of scientific discourse, with which they develop scientific knowledge and understanding. The teacher is a facilitator for this entry into a scientific discourse community, and scientific literacy is achieved by students with control of this important secondary discourse.

Blurring and Crossing the Boundaries of Tradition

In all three of the traditions above it is our intent to use commonplaces to highlight differences in the perspectives each takes on the case of Jennifer and Juan. Regardless of which research tradition one most identifies with, the response to Jennifer's situation involves constructing a better understanding of the situation, especially of Juan as a student, and making use of that understanding as a basis for further interaction and teaching. Other chapters within this book provide excellent illustrations of how those with strategies and discourse orientations go about constructing this understanding and making use of it. In order to contribute, one of our goals is to help illustrate a content-oriented approach to understanding such a situation. Yet, before we do this, we feel it is important to note the ways in which the research traditions can and do inform each other in some productive ways.

So far in this chapter we have attempted to categorize research broadly for the purpose of examining differences in the ways the research community considers literacy. Yet our intent is not to suggest that such boundaries are fixed and nonporous. In fact, within the science education research community there is a growing concern for the treatment of literacy, as well as an understanding of how literacy research and science education research intersect. In claiming that literacy in the "fundamental sense" (i.e., reading and writing) is "central to scientific literacy," Norris and Phillips (2003) seek to open a greater dialogue between what we refer to as content- and strategies-oriented researchers. Likewise, other scholars are finding ways to bridge the gaps between these orientations and to blend notions of text, scientific reasoning, and content understanding. For example, a series of researchers have offered reading protocols that have sought to improve learning through reading (e.g., Dansereau, 1985; Palincsar, 1986; Spiegel & Barufaldi, 1994). Specifically, Spiegel and Barufaldi's (1994) work suggested that construction of graphic postorganizers would significantly improve students' recall and comprehension abilities in science.

Research on writing in science classrooms is also providing connections between content- and strategies-oriented traditions. As an example, Keys, Hand, Prain, and Collins (1999) report that students can generate meaning with evidence regarding specific scientific topics, make connections between observations and inferences, and develop metacognitive awareness about writing in science. An increasing amount of research on writing in science education has created a growing body of knowledge (e.g., Hand, Prain, Lawrence, & Yore, 1999; Holliday, Yore, & Alvermann, 1994; Keys, 1999). The focus of this research is increasingly integrating studies of written and spoken classroom text (e.g., Keys, 1997; Rivard & Straw, 2000), thus highlighting the importance of multiple modes of language use. Despite such studies addressing writing in science, the most significant concern for the bridging of content- and strategies-oriented research is in regards to issues of context. Rivard (1994) explored this issue, suggesting that decontextualized studies of writing lack "ecological validity" (p. 975). Researchers from both strategies- and content-oriented perspectives are beginning to raise similar concerns for studies of reading and speaking within science classrooms and the ways in which multiple modes of communication mix together in students' understanding of science.

In order to address such concerns, researchers are increasingly blurring the boundaries between content- and discourse-orientations with some interesting results. For example, Vellom and Anderson (1999), as a result of their study of classroom discourse around the concept of density, caution that learning science "must consist of inquiry and problem solving based on direct experience with phenomena" (p. 180), while also considering the social and cultural factors that mediate student interaction. In their work on classroom discourse, O'Connor and Michaels examine the ways in which "the literacies of home and school are not always congruent" (1993, p. 318). Similarly, Gallego and Hollingsworth suggest that personal literacies are different from school literacies, and they reflect how students "believe they should join in socially accepted discourse communities and the private ways they know they can and would like to be able to participate" (2000, p. 15).

Recognizing and examining the spaces between more disciplinary-specific literacies (e.g., science literacy) and those of students' cultures can provide fertile ground for discussion and collaboration between content-, strategies-, and discourse-oriented researchers. Such collaborations may prompt changes in each tradition that would bridge divides even more. For example, in their examination of what they call "everyday sense-making," Warren, Ballenger, Ogonowski, Rosebery, and Hudicourt-Barnes (2001) suggest that ways of knowing in other cultures may be in conflict with those of science. Additionally, they push for the broadening of science classroom discourse to include more ways of knowing so that more students are able to express their conceptions. One reaction of a content- or strategies-oriented researcher or practitioner might be to dismiss such claims as troublesome or complicating. Yet, by allowing a fuller discussion of what counts as *scientific* in the science classroom— and who can participate in sense making—we allow for conversations about precisely those aspects of the curriculum (e.g., inquiry, method, evidence-based reasoning) that we hold so dear. Moreover, classroom conversations would allow more students to engage in the metacognitive strategies around different kinds of sense making. As a result of such border crossing (or border blurring), it may be possible to consider a hybrid definition of scientific literacy; scientifically literate students engage in communities of practice that employ strategies for creating and using texts that foster agency in the material world.

Just as content-oriented researchers and practitioners can learn a great deal from the different perspectives, strategies- and discourse-oriented researchers are already aware of science as a fertile ground for future work on literacy. Gee suggests that "all of literacy education has a great deal to learn from scientific literacy" (2004, p. 42) in light of the regular multimodality of texts in science: charts, diagrams, and equations, as well as a strong presence of expository texts. Gee makes a strong case for considering a broad range of texts in science classrooms:

> We need to devote more explicit attention to teaching students how to read hybrid text. We need to help them understand the conventions that connect verbal text with mathematical expressions and graphs and diagrams of all kinds. We need to help them reproduce the fusion of conceptual kinds and quantitative degrees that is central to scientific meaning-making by giving them practice in translating back and forth among verbal accounts, mathematical expressions and calculations, schematic diagrams, abstract graphs, and hands-on actions. (p. 41)

It is this idea that motivates the next section of the chapter: a closer look at the content-oriented perspective and the potential benefit in examining scientific texts for literacy research.

CONTENT-ORIENTED CRITIQUES AND SCIENTIFIC TEXTS

Our framework in Table 7.1 attempts to portray three research traditions in terms of four commonplaces in discussions about scientific literacy. We followed this with examples of each tradition—content-, strategies-, and discourse-oriented research—and likely responses to Jennifer's question from each, based on how we see them. Part of opening dialogue between research traditions involves understanding the ways in which each perspective might view others. To this end, and keeping in mind our backgrounds as science content-oriented researchers, we will now try to provide some examples of the concerns that occur to us as we examine the other two perspectives. We will follow this up with a more detailed examination of content-oriented notions of scientific texts and reasoning. These discussions are meant as a means for increasing understanding (ours, as well as our readers') of different research traditions.

From the content-oriented perspective, the focus on written texts (as per the strategies orientation) is problematic for two main reasons. First, adopting a vision of literacy that primarily focuses on improving the ways in which students interrogate written texts suggests placing a diminished value on interaction with the material world. Second, there is a great deal of concern over the quality of the texts—especially commercially produced curricula (Kesidou & Roseman, 2002)—that currently are in use in science classrooms. It is our hope that a search for improved literacy strategies also would involve a serious examination of the texts that are in use.

Similarly, a content-oriented researcher or practitioner would have concerns in regards to the discourse-oriented suggestions offered to Jennifer. First, much of the context upon which the differences between discourses (home and science) depend is out of the immediate control of teachers and other practitioners. Moreover, the complexity of discourse-oriented practices is such that implementation is often difficult to negotiate for well-versed scholars, let alone novice teachers. If Jennifer were to try, for example, creating a hybrid space for Juan, it is less likely that she would understand how to do this at the level of daily practice than at a broader, holistic level. Though helpful in understanding how discourse operates within specific classroom contexts, discourse-oriented research tends to be less helpful in suggesting means for fostering specific kinds of discourse in specific classroom contexts.

In light of these concerns, it is important to understand the motivations of a content-oriented researcher or practitioner a bit better. The importance placed on experience in the material world in content-oriented science education tends to have two main consequences. First, there is less of a focus on human-generated expository texts in favor of spending more time engaged with the material world. This is not to say that such texts are unimportant from the content-oriented perspective, but these texts do not take precedence as they might from another perspective. The second consequence of the centrality of the material world in the content-oriented perspective on science literacy is a decreased attention to the social and cultural aspects of teaching and learning.

Toward the aim of closing gaps between research traditions, we suggest *better texts*—that is, texts that (1) mediate students' interactions with the material world and (2) introduce students to the ways in which scientists create and use texts. These two goals frame the brief discussion that follows: regarding the ways that scientific texts can play a role in student interaction with the material world and what such texts might look like.

Scientific communities depend on texts to communicate for any number of purposes, and all are developed through highly integrated literacy practices. Many of the typical genres are quite familiar to researchers and practitioners (e.g., reports, journal articles, laboratory notebooks), though all may not have ready counterparts within a classroom setting. Even so, there are many scientific texts that do appear in both scientific and science classroom communities. Graphs, diagrams, databases, pictures, simulations, model-based analyses, equations, and data-pattern explanations are a few examples of texts that content-oriented researchers and practitioners would consider as targets for literacy development in science. It is important to note that these are not unique to science—mathematics and social studies teachers might consider many of these central to their work as well. These kinds of texts are particularly useful for making scientific arguments and engaging in scientific practices. But what do such arguments and practices look like?

Scientists create arguments to make sense of the world by finding connections among observations, patterns, and theoretical models. Our understanding of the nature of scientific arguments and practices is represented in Figure 7.1. Let us start from the bottom of Figure 7.1, considering each aspect.

• *Observations or data.* Scientists know the world only through their interactions with it—through perceptual and intellectual experience in the material world. Scientists choose to concentrate on experiences that they can verify, reproduce, describe or measure precisely, record, and communicate to others; these are the experiences that they call "observations" or "data." Thus scientists are constantly seeking to

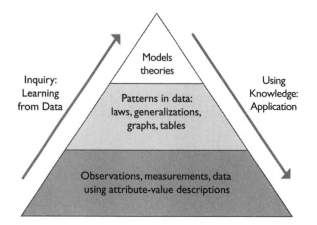

FIGURE 7.1. A model for scientific practices. From Michigan Department of Education (2007). Copyright 2007 by Michigan Department of Education. Reprinted by permission.

create new experiences and to select and refine them into data suitable for pattern finding. Descriptions of individual plants or animals, individual measurements denoted by points on a graph, weather reports, and readings from particle detectors in cyclotrons are all experiences that scientists would consider data. They work hard to make sure that their observations are tied as closely as possible to the phenomena (events) and systems of the material world. The broad base of Figure 7.1 represents the idea that scientific knowledge is based on many (and many types of) experiences; most scientists spend a large part of their professional lives accumulating experience (i.e., collecting data) in some small portion of the material world and sharing their data with other scientists.

   • *Patterns in data* (*laws, generalizations, graphs, tables*). Scientific laws and generalizations are statements about patterns that scientists see when interpreting their data. The gas laws, for example, present patterns of relationships among the temperature, pressure, and volume of gases that encompass millions of individual measurements (observations) that scientists have made over the years. Thus pattern finding is a central scientific practice. Graphs and data tables are ways of presenting data (i.e., organizing experience) so that others (usually readers) can see the patterns. These patterns in experience are important links between data and theories.

   • *Scientific models and theories.* Scientific models and theories are designed to explain patterns in data. For example, biologists accept the

theory of evolution because it explains many different patterns that scientists have observed in different ways—in the fossil record, in changes
in populations observed by humans, in the biochemical makeup of different organisms, and so forth. To continue with a previous example,
the patterns in experience that we call the gas laws do not explain *why*
gases behave the way they do, but kinetic molecular *theory* does. In fact,
kinetic molecular theory explains why the gas laws are the way they are
in addition to explaining many other patterns. The most well-known
scientific theories are beautiful in the elegant and parsimonious way
that they explain a "diversity of phenomena." Scientific models are sim-
pler versions of theories that explain a smaller set of patterns. For example, a "billiard ball model" of a gas explains the patterns summarized
in the gas laws rather well, but not why gases sometimes condense into
liquids (which kinetic molecular theory does explain). The small tip of
Figure 7.1 indicates that the power of scientific theories and models lies
in their parsimony—a few theories can explain many different patterns,
each of which is based on very large numbers of observations.

In Figure 7.1, the arrows represent the key scientific practices
(each actually a complex set of related practices): inquiry and application. Our present scientific knowledge is the product of generations of
scientific inquiry. Scientific inquiry is worthwhile, though, only because the
knowledge that it produces is useful. Thus the practices of application—
using scientific knowledge to describe, explain, predict, or design phenomena and systems in the material world—are as important as the
practices of inquiry. Scientific application and inquiry have been ex-
traordinarily successful in shaping our culture and society; scientists
have built up a large and powerful array of experiences, patterns, and
explanations. These practices are among the most important kinds of
scientific practices; as a result, they get the most attention in standards
documents (American Association for the Advancement of Science,
1990, 1993; National Research Council, 1996, 2000), written from a
content-oriented perspective. We have made science a school subject, in
no small part, because of the benefits that society derives from scientific
inquiry and application. Therefore, as the content-oriented perspective
sees it, if we want students to share in the benefits of science, helping
them learn and make use of those practices is central to the goal of scientific literacy.

Our aim, then, regarding the use of scientific texts in schools is to
promote them as tools for analyzing, describing, and understanding the
material world, which are ongoing practices in scientific communities.

Whether the text is a bulleted list of characteristics from a course text-book or the reading of a thermometer in a laboratory activity, it is important to enrich and expand the ways students make use of them to understand the material world. However, in science classrooms, there is often a thin line between using texts as tools to engage in practices like inquiry or application, and translating texts entirely into "facts for learning" (often read as memorization). Though knowing things about the material world is an admirable goal, the thin line is crossed all too often so that demonstrating understanding of science becomes an act of recalling discrete bits of content without consideration for reasoning about the material world. An example of this distinction may help to clear up the difference between these two uses of a scientific text.

As a result of increased public awareness, Figure 7.2 may appear quite familiar: it is a graphical representation of global temperature deviation from the years 1880 to 2000 C.E. As a scientific text, it represents both a data display and a potential site of inquiry practices. First, this could be used to establish the "fact" of global climate change. A noticeable trend occurs within the graph, and a statement such as "Global temperature appears to be increasing in an alarming manner" is one possible "fact" to be learned from it. Though it may be important in helping to raise awareness of environmental issues, this translation-to-fact is far from the only practice this text can support. Choosing to see this graph as a representation of patterns in data, a host of potential inquiry practices can be pursued. From analyzing the relationships between specific points on the graph (perhaps to consider changes over time), to investigating ways in which such data might be collected, to describing the relationship between annual and 5-year mean curves, this graph holds more potential as a text than as one singular, holistic interpretation.

In order to foster these sorts of rich scientific practices, teachers and students make use of such scientific texts through inquiry and application. Therefore, looking beyond science textbooks toward the material world as a source of scientific text is an important goal for expanding the conversation about literacy in the content area of science, precisely because of the context of science. Whether interpreting patterns and potential explanations from material world observations (i.e., inquiry) or making use of scientific models to understand specific phenomena (i.e., application), the scientific text is a central part of doing and learning science. Such texts involve not only measurements and instruments for observation, but also the social and cultural (as well as rhetorical) choices made in the process of producing and interpreting

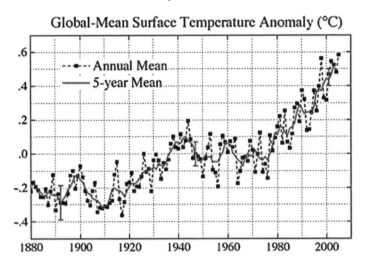

FIGURE 7.2. A graph as scientific text. From *www.climate.org/topics/climate/2005hot. shtml.* Copyright by the Climate Institute. Reprinted by permission.

them. As a result, developing students' agency with scientific texts— that is, their ability to reason with these texts in scientific ways—is a goal that involves insights from all three research traditions. Therefore, we hope to communicate across traditions about the important goal of scientific literacy in our work with science teacher candidates.

DIRECTIONS FOR FUTURE RESEARCH

In the discussion of all three of the traditions it is our intent to use commonplaces to highlight differences in the perspectives each takes on the case of Jennifer and Juan. By examining these differences we can better articulate the ways in which *we* might answer Jennifer's question. We can also consider ramifications for our work as teacher educators and educational researchers.

We know that telling Jennifer our answers will not be enough. Regardless of which research tradition a teacher educator most identifies with, the response to Jennifer's situation likely involves constructing a better understanding of the situation, especially of Juan as a student, and making use of that understanding as a basis for further interaction and teaching. Yet this is no small feat, especially for teacher candidates. We realize, as teacher educators, that we need to do something similar with our students—we need to construct a better understanding of how our teacher candidates see their roles, their students, the nature of scientific literacy, and science texts. Along with our colleagues at Michigan State University, we are beginning this process in our work.

Though in its infancy, our research is allowing us to find better vantage points from which to consider the perspectives and experiences of the teacher candidates in our science teacher preparation program. We have conducted individual and small-group interviews with current students from multiple points in our program. Presenting them with three different cases—a clinical interview with an individual student, an example lesson from an experienced teacher, and a tutoring session between a student and a teacher candidate—we asked the teacher candidates about their perspectives on the four commonplaces within the context of each case. Though this kind of video casework is not new (cf. Rosebery & Warren, 1996), our hope is that the variety of cases we present to candidates will allow for more nuanced views of their notions of teaching, students, subject matter, and texts. After transcribing the videotaped interviews, we have started looking at the data and are beginning to find some very striking results.

The videos of teaching we have used show varying but rich examples of teaching, yet teacher candidates do not seem able to unpack what they observe. For example, the teacher candidates we interviewed seem to understand the students primarily through the lens of their own experiences as learners. This sometimes works well for developing teachers, but rarely with learners like Juan whose experiences are substantially different from theirs. In seeing the way they are responding to these videos we realize that we (as their instructors) must be wary of the same sort of limited perspective; we need a model of how our preservice teachers understand and think about teaching science as a basis for how we teach them.

Since they rely on themselves as models of learners, teacher candidates often seem not to notice what the teachers do in each case to understand students (i.e., the process of constructing a better model of students or modifying instruction to meet student-specific needs). The teacher candidates talk more about what actions the teacher takes and whether/how the students respond than about what students say and bring into the situation. In a way, teacher candidates appear to see teaching as more about what can be done *to* students and less about what students possess and can do already. As evidence of this, the teacher candidates' comments frequently lack any clear differentiation between what students know and how they respond to questions. They frequently speak of student misconceptions and ways to remediate them, but without indicating they are paying attention to the experiences and reasoning *behind* the views held by students.

With regards to notions of literacy and texts, we have noticed something interesting as we continue to analyze transcripts and engage in conversations with colleagues. We are gaining valuable insight into the dialogue between teacher candidates and science education instructors. The transcripts provide evidence that teacher candidates incorporate more of the language and ideas presented in their education courses as they progress in the program. The candidates and their science teacher education instructors share a focus on the material world as the most important text for a science classroom, and on how students and teachers make use of phenomena rather than how they interact with written texts. As a result, the dialogue is centered on a content-oriented perspective and often lacks components of both strategies- and discourse-oriented perspectives on scientific literacy.

Even so, the importance that interviewees place on material world experience in teaching seems tempered by the perception of these as useful primarily for persuading students of the "correct" narratives found in curricula and textbooks. As a result, many of the interviewees share grudging acceptance of the need for science textbooks while downplaying their value for most students, mostly due to the texts' low interest value or students' difficulty with comprehension.

In terms of text production, the candidates often mention student writing as a means for assessment of understanding, though little connection is made between students' writing and scientists' knowledge production. When the candidates talk about assessing students' prior knowledge, they speak more of misconceptions than of intellectual resources. Again, given the content-oriented perspective of most of their science teaching methods courses, the absence of either strategies- or discourse-oriented ideas about texts and literacy is not entirely unexpected.

This is where our work stands at this point. Our expectations are that through consideration of teachers candidates' perspectives on the same commonplaces we will be in a much better position to help them take advantage of the knowledge that the three traditions have to offer. It is our aim not to focus on science as information (i.e., a science master narrative), but instead on science as a sociocultural, conceptual toolkit for inquiry, explaining, and predicting, suggesting a fusion of content, strategies, and discourse orientations. In order to meet the demands of this fusion of orientations, we need to extend our work to include methods and ideas that are respectful and inclusive of *all three* traditions, and some which are accessible (and practical) to our teacher candidates like Jennifer.

In order to meet these demands, our ongoing work seeks to achieve several ends. We continue to make connections among the three perspectives on literacy in science as portrayed above: content-, strategies- and discourse-oriented. We are also exploring ways to help teacher candidates consider responsive models of teaching based on connected orientations toward students and literacy in science. We also hope to extend this connection within the sciences to include connections between mathematics, science, and literacy research. Also, from a practical stance, it is our hope that this work will improve teacher preparation courses by interrelating these disciplines.

Even as our work continues, we hope others might see similar areas for potential research. Partnerships between content- and strategies-oriented researchers can continue to investigate the central role of scientific texts as tools for representing and analyzing the material world. Similarly, discourse- and content-oriented research could further examine the ways that scientific textual genres and representational forms operate in classroom communities of practice (e.g., graphs, databases, simulations). Combining and comparing the decoding and interpreting of such texts with the decoding and interpreting of systems and processes in the material world (perhaps treating it as a kind of hybrid text itself) might provide other interesting intersections between strategies- and content-oriented research programs, while also contributing to our understandings of students' reasoning in science. Also, continuing to create classroom communities of practice where students engage in the purpose of representing and analyzing the material world is a site where all three traditions can contribute a great deal. Each of these possible directions for research would benefit the larger community.

CONCLUSION

We started this chapter with a discussion of three research traditions. Content-oriented, strategies-oriented, and discourse-oriented researchers all have important insights into how students learn from texts and from "the Book of Nature." We have used commonplaces as the basis for conversation about scientific literacy, as well as avenues for improving the research and practices within science teacher education. It is our hope that by providing a framework for conversations about the nature of scientific texts, the role of the teacher, ideas about student learning, and the goal of scientifically literate learners, a continuing dialogue will make room for further research and improve our practice as science teacher educators.

All three research traditions involve care for the student as a reader, writer, and learner, even though each may focus on different aspects of the situation and go about constructing models of students and their learning in different ways. For content-oriented researchers, the primary focus of the model is how the student interacts with and interprets the material world. For strategies-oriented researchers, the model of the student is focused more on how the student interacts with human-generated texts with an array of strategies or schemata that he or she brings to bear on the texts. For the discourse-oriented researcher, the primary concern is how the student interacts with explicit and implicit discourse communities and social groups. In each tradition there are methods and practices that can benefit those learning to teach science. So, whether confronted with Jennifer's dilemma, the developing ideas of other teacher candidates, or potential avenues for future research, continuing the literacy conversation in science is to the benefit of us all.

REFERENCES

Alvermann, D. E. (2001). *Effective literacy instruction for adolescents* (Executive Summary and Paper Commissioned by the National Reading Conference). Chicago: National Reading Conference.

American Association for the Advancement of Science. (1990). *Science for all Americans*. New York: Author.

American Association for the Advancement of Science. (1993). *Benchmarks for science literacy*. New York: Oxford University Press.

Barton, A., & Yang, K. (2000). The culture of power and science education: Learning from Miguel. *Journal of Research in Science Teaching, 37*(8), 871–889.

Bazerman, C. (1988). *Shaping written knowledge: The genre and activity of the experimental article in science*. Madison: University of Wisconsin Press.

Champagne, A. B., Lovitts, B. E., & Calinger, B. J. (Eds.). (1989). *Scientific literacy*. Washington, DC: American Association for the Advancement of Science.

Conant, J. B. (1952). *Modern science and modern man*. New York: Columbia University Press.

Crease, R. P. (2006, December). The book of nature. *Physics World*. Retrieved from *physicsweb.org/articles/world/19/12/4/1*

Dansereau, D. F. (1985). Learning strategy research. In J. W. Segal, S. F. Chapman, & R. Glaser (Eds.), *Thinking and learning skills: Vol. 1. Relating instruction to research* (pp. 209–239). Hillsdale: Erlbaum.

Deshler, D. D., Hock, M. F., & Catts, H. (2006). Enhancing outcomes for struggling adolescent readers. *IDA Perspectives, 10*(2), 21–26.

Deshler, D. D., Schumaker, J., Harris, K. R., & Graham, S. (Eds.). (1999). *Teaching every adolescent every day: Learning in diverse middle and high school classrooms.* Cambridge, MA: Brookline Books.

Deshler, D. D., & Tollefson, J. (2006). Strategic interventions for struggling adolescent learners. *School Administrator, 63*(4), 24–30.

Dole, J., Duffy, G., Roehler, L., & Pearson, P. (1991). Moving from the old to the new: Research on reading comprehension instruction. *Review of Educational Research, 61,* 239–264.

Driver, R., Squires, A., Rushworth, P., & Wood-Robinson, V. (1994). *Making sense of secondary science: Research into children's ideas.* New York: Routledge.

Duit, R. (2007). Bibliography: Students' and teachers' conceptions and science education. Retrieved February 12, 2007, from *www.ipn.uni-kiel.de/aktuell/stcse/download_stcse.html*

Duke, N. K., Purcell-Gates, V., Hall, L. A., & Tower, C. (2006–2007). Authentic literacy activities for developing comprehension and writing. *Reading Teacher, 60,* 344–355.

Duschl, R. (2003). The assessment of argumentation and explanation: Creating and supporting teachers' feedback strategies. In D. Zeidler (Ed.), *The role of moral reasoning on socio-scientific issues and discourse in science education* (pp. 131–161). Dordrecht, The Netherlands: Kluwer Academic.

Fang, Z. (2004). Scientific literacy: A systemic functional linguistics perspective. *Science Education, 89,* 335–347.

Gallego, M. A., & Hollingsworth, S. (Eds.). (2000). *What counts as literacy?: Challenging the school standard.* New York: Teachers College Press.

Gaskins, I. W., & Pressley, M. (2007). Teaching metacognitive strategies that address executive-function processes within a schoolwide curriculum. In L. Meltzer (Ed.), *Executive function in education: From theory to practice* (pp. 261–286). New York: Guilford Press.

Gee, J. P. (1991). What is literacy? In C. W. Mitchell & K. Weiler (Eds.), *Rewriting literacy: Culture and the discourse of the other* (pp. 3–12). New York: Bergin & Garvey.

Gee, J. P. (2004). Language in the science classroom: Academic social languages as the heart of school-based literacy. In E. W. Saul (Ed.), *Crossing borders in literacy and science instruction: Perspectives on theory and practice* (pp. 13–32). Newark, DE: International Reading Association and National Science Teachers Association.

Gersten, R., Fuchs, L., Williams, J., & Baker, S. (2001). Teaching reading comprehension strategies to students with learning disabilities: A review of research. *Review of Educational Research, 71,* 279–320.

Halliday, M. A. K., & Martin, J. R. (Eds.). (1993). *Writing science: Literacy and discursive power.* Pittsburgh, PA: University of Pittsburgh Press.

Hand, B., Prain, V., Lawrence, C., & Yore, L. D. (1999). A writing in science framework designed to improve science literacy. *International Journal of Science Education, 10,* 1021–1036.

Hock, M. F., Schumaker, J. B., & Deshler, D. D. (2001). The case for strategic tutoring. *Educational Leadership, 58*(7), 50–52.

Holliday, W. G., Yore, L. D., & Alvermann, D. E. (1994). The reading–science learning–writing connection: Breakthroughs, barriers, and promises. *Journal of Research in Science Teaching, 31*(9), 877–893.

Hurd, P. (1958). Science literacy: Its meaning for American schools. *Educational Leadership, 16,* 13–16.

Jimnez-Aleixandre, M. P., Rodrigues, A. B., & Duschl, R. A. (2000). "Doing the lesson" or "doing science": Argument in high school genetics. *Science Education, 84*(6), 757–792.

Kamil, M. (2003). *Adolescents and literacy: Reading for the 21st century.* Washington, DC: Alliance for Excellent Education.

Kesidou, S., & Roseman, J. E. (2002). How well do middle school science programs measure up?: Findings from Project 2061's curriculum review. *Journal of Research in Science Teaching, 39*(6), 522–549.

Keys, C. (1997). An investigation of the relationship between scientific reasoning, conceptual knowledge and model formulation in a naturalistic setting. *International Journal of Science Education, 19,* 957–970.

Keys, C. W. (1999). Revitalizing instruction in scientific genres: Connecting knowledge production with writing to learn in science. *Science Education, 83,* 115–130.

Keys, C. W., Hand, B., Prain, V., & Collins, S. (1999). Using the science writing heuristic as a tool for learning from laboratory investigations in secondary science. *Journal of Research in Science Teaching, 36,* 1065–1081.

Lee, S., & Roth, W.-M. (2003). Of traversals and hybrid spaces: Science in the community. *Mind, Culture, and Activity, 10*(2), 120–142.

Lemke, J. (1990). *Talking science: Language, learning, and values.* Norwood, NJ: Ablex.

Lemke, J. (2001). Foreword. In J. Wellington & J. Osborne (Eds.), *Language and literacy in science education* (pp. iv–v). Philadelphia: Open University Press.

Martin, J. R., & Veel, R. (1998). *Reading science: Critical and functional perspectives on discourses of science.* New York: Routledge.

McCurdy, R. C. (1958). Towards a population literate in science. *The Science Teacher, 25,* 366–368.

Michaels, S., & O'Connor, M. C. (1991). *Literacy as reasoning within multiple discourses: Implications for policy and educational reform.* Paper presented at the Council of Chief State School Officers 1990 Summer Institute.

Michigan Department of Education. (2007). *High school science content expectations.* Lansing: Michigan Department of Education.

Moje, E. B., Collazo, T., Carrillo, R., & Marx, R. W. (2001). "Maestro, what is 'quality'?": Language, literacy, and discourse in project-based science. *Journal of Research in Science Teaching, 38*(4), 469–498.

Moore, D. W., Bean, T. W., Birdyshaw, D., & Rycik, J. A. (1999). Adolescent literacy: A position statement. *Journal of Adolescent and Adult Literacy, 43,* 97–112.

National Research Council. (1996). *National science education standards.* Washington, DC: National Academy Press.

National Research Council. (2000). *Inquiry and the national science education standards: A guide for teaching and learning.* Washington, DC: National Academy Press.

Norris, S. P., & Phillips, L. M. (2003). How literacy in its fundamental sense is central to scientific literacy. *Science Education, 87*(2), 224–240.

O'Connor, M. C., & Michaels, S. (1993). Aligning academic task and participation status through revoicing: Analysis of a classroom discourse strategy. *Anthropology and Education Quarterly, 24*(4), 318–335.

Palincsar, A. S. (1986). *Reciprocal teaching: Teaching reading as thinking.* Oak Brook, IL: North Central Regional Educational Laboratory.

Popper, K. (1972). *Objective knowledge: An evolutionary approach.* Oxford, UK: Clarendon Press.

Purcell-Gates, V., Duke, N. K., & Martineau, J. A. (2007). Learning to read and write genre-specific text: Roles of authentic experience and explicit teaching. *Reading Research Quarterly, 42,* 8–45.

Rivard, L. P. (2004). Are language-based activities in science effective for all students, including low achievers? *Science Education, 88*(3), 420–442.

Rivard, L. P., & Straw, S. B. (2000). The effect of talk and writing on learning science: An exploratory study. *Science Education, 84*(5), 566–593.

Rosebery, A., & Warren, B. (1996). *Sense making science.* Portsmith, NH: Heinemann.

Roth, W.-M. (2004). Gestures: The leading edge in literacy development. In E. W. Saul (Ed.), *Crossing borders in literacy and science instruction: Perspectives on theory and practice* (pp. 48–67). Newark, DE: International Reading Association & National Science Teachers Association.

Roth, W.-M., McRobbie, C. J., Lucas, K. B., & Boutonne, S. (1997). The local production of order in traditional science laboratories: A phenomenological analysis. *Learning and Instruction, 7*(2), 107–136.

Rutherford, F. J., & Ahlgren, A. (1990). *Science for all Americans.* New York: Oxford University Press.

Schwab, J. (1969). The practical: A language for curriculum. *School Review, 78*(1), 1–23.

Spiegel, G. F., & Barufaldi, J. P. (1994). The effects of a combination of text structure awareness and graphic postorganizers on recall and retention of science knowledge. *Journal of Research in Science Teaching, 31,* 913–932.

Veel, R. (1997). Learning how to mean—scientifically speaking: Apprenticeship into scientific discourse in the secondary school. In F. Christie & J. R. Martin (Eds.), *Genre and institutions: Social processes in the workplace and school* (pp. 161–195). London: Cassell.

Vellom, P., & Anderson, C. W. (1999). Reasoning about data in middle school contexts. *Journal of Research in Science Teaching, 36*(2), 179–199.

Warren, B., Ballenger, C., Ogonowski, M., Rosebery, A., & Hudicourt-Barnes, J. (2001). Rethinking diversity in learning science: The logic of everyday sensemaking. *Journal of Research in Science Teaching, 38*(5), 529–552.

Wellington, J., & Osborne, J. (2001). *Language and literacy in science education.* Philadelphia: Open University Press.

Zembal-Saul, C., Krajcik, J., & Blumenfeld, P. (2002). Elementary student teachers' science content representations. *Journal of Research in Science Teaching, 39,* 443–463.

8

Literacy Coaching

CATHY M. ROLLER

Not much has changed with literacy coaching research since Snow, Ippilito, and Schwarz (2006) commented, " . . . our knowledge consists primarily of case studies and practitioner results rather than systematic study" (p. 44). However, we must not underestimate the importance of that work to establishing a research base for literacy coaching. We should take seriously their statement:

> The coaching model being widely adopted is consistent with research evidence concerning effective professional development. That evidence suggests that local, site-specific, instructionally focused, ongoing professional development generally works better than the traditional pull-out models focused on school-wide or district-wide issues (Guskey, 2000). The coaches' role, though somewhat variable across sites, generally includes designing and implementing these preferred professional development models by facilitating the work of ongoing collaborative teacher groups, centering the collaborative work on shared instructional challenges, promoting demonstration lessons and cross-classroom observations, and developing opportunities to inspect students' performance on tests and in-class assignments so as to inform instruction. (p. 35)

THE RESEARCH WE HAVE

The case studies we have are generally evaluations of whole-school and sometimes of whole-district and even statewide interventions that use coaching as a component. For example, the America's Choice model has had a number of evaluations (May, Supovitz, & Lesnick, 2004; May, Supovitz, & Perda, 2004; Poglinco et al., 2003; Supovitz & May, 2003; Supovitz & Taylor, 2003). We could cite similar series of reports for Success for All (Success for All Foundation, 2006) and other models that use coaching as a major component. There are similar documents for Montgomery County, Maryland, the State of South Carolina (Deford et al., 2003; South Carolina Research Initiative, 2002); Boston, Massachusetts, public schools (Schwartz & McCarthy, 2003), and the San Diego Unified School District (Galm & Perry, 2004).

The list could go on and on. The general finding in all of these case studies is that interventions built on coaching models can be successful in raising achievement—although there is considerable variation from school to school. The level of implementation is a factor correlating with the level of success. This data probably passes the man-on-the-street test—a reasonable person could conclude that literacy coaching is likely to increase reading achievement given that it is well implemented.

Several models of coaching have a stronger research base. Costa and Garmston (2002, p. 5) describe cognitive coaching as "a simple model for conversations about planning, reflecting or problem solving. At deeper levels, it serves as the nucleus for professional communities that honor autonomy, encourage independence, and produce high achievement. Greene (2004, p. 4) summarizes cognitive coaching as supporting "the examination of a teacher's own professional practice through self-examination of 'familiar patterns of practice and underlying assumptions that guide and direct action' (Costa & Garmston, 2002, p. 5)." Studies of cognitive coaching indicate that coached teachers are directly impacted and change behaviors to a greater degree than uncoached teachers.

Cognitive coaching has been examined in relation to teacher efficacy. Studies point to benefits for students based on improvements in teacher efficacy (Greene, 2004, p. 5). In addition, there is some evidence that cognitive coaching impacts students. Grinder (1996) reported significant advantages for children taught by coached teachers as opposed to those whose teachers did not receive coaching. They reported effects on Total Iowa Test of Basic Skills (ITBS) Scores and Integrated Writing Total Score as well as effects on several ITBS Mathematics scores.

Joyce and Showers designed studies to investigate the impact of continued assistance in the form of coaching following initial training of new content. They found that coaching facilitated transfer of training (as cited in Greene, 2004, p. 7). Greene in fact cites several models of effective coaching including:

- Content-focused coaching (West & Staub, 2003)
- Professional development framework (Lyons & Pinnell, 2001)
- Gradual release of responsibility model (Pearson & Gallagher, 1983)
- Intentional teaching model and reflective coaching (Rock, 2002)
- Coaching in study groups and book clubs (Walpole & McKenna, 2004)

Another interesting set of research evidence comes from a series of workshops on adolescent literacy supported by the National Institute for Child Health and Human Development, the American Federation of Teachers, the American Speech and Hearing Association, the International Reading Association, the National Education Association, the National Institute for Literacy, and four offices of the Department of Education: Vocational and Adult Education, Educational Research and Improvement, Elementary and Secondary Education, and Special Education and Rehabilitation Services. After conducting a research meeting to sketch the outlines of existing research on adolescent literacy and noting areas that lacked form and definition, the organization held a more practice-oriented workshop that focused on four existing intervention programs: the corrective reading model developed by SRA/McGraw Hill; The *Language!* model developed by Sopris West Educational Services, Longmont, California; the strategic reading course model that is an instructional component of the Talent Development High School developed at Johns Hopkins University; and the strategic instruction model developed at the Kansas Center for Research on Learning. Dr. Peggy McCardle emphasized the point that the four models were selected to demonstrate a process of examination, brainstorming, improvement, and research regarding effectiveness. What is interesting about the four selected models is that all four models rely on job-embedded coaching.

In addition to the case studies and evaluations, we are beginning to see descriptions of reading/literacy coaching across sites. For example, Richard (2003) provides a monograph from the Edna McConnell Clark Foundation that relies on interviews of staff developers, principals, teachers, and others in the following places: Long Beach and San Diego, California; Montgomery County, Maryland; Bolivar, County, Mississippi; as well as the author's reviews of research and case studies. The Aspen Institute Program on Education and the Annenberg Institute for School Reform published *Coaching: A Strategy for Developing Instructional Capacity* (Neufield & Roper, 2003). Their analysis is based primarily on longitudinal, qualitative studies in Boston; Corpus Christi, Texas; Louisville, Kentucky; and San Diego. These authors conclude that while coaching has not yet been "proven to increase student achievement, [it] does increase the instructional capacity of schools and teachers, a known prerequisite for increasing learning" (p. v). In addition, we are beginning to see descriptions of coaches and coaching from the Reading First implementations around the nation. Several surveys such as the one published by the International Reading Association in *Reading Today* provide descriptions of reading/literacy coaches. In conclusion, the survey provided a description of reading/literacy coaches as teachers who work primarily with teachers and spend a significant portion of their time in assessment and instructional planning activities. They spend little time evaluating teachers or working directly with students. The most typical reported job requirements are a BA and 1–3 years of teaching experience with some emphasis on communications skills, presentation skills, and group facilitation skills.

Another important addition to the research is the evaluations of the Striving Readers Grants awarded by the U.S. Department of Education. The implementation began in September 2006, and each project was required to use an experimental or quasi-experimental evaluation design. The projects are now up and running, and they have been successful in initiating experimental designs to evaluate the remedial intervention programs and in initiating the quasi-experimental designs to evaluate whole-school efforts. At present none of the evaluation designs includes a component to examine the coaching that is going on. However, the programs and the U.S. Department of Education have found that coaching is going on in most or all of the programs and they are very hopeful about adding research questions related to coaching to the evaluation designs (M. Kingman, personal communication, October 18, 2006).

In addition, the International Reading Association has developed both a position statement and *Standards for Middle and High School Literacy Coaches* (2006b). The position statement, *The Role and Qualifications of the Reading Coach in the United States* (2004), defines the role of the reading coach; describes what a reading coach should know and be able to do; and provides recommendations for policymakers, school administrators, reading specialists, reading coaches, and classroom teachers. The association states:

> Reading coaches have great potential to provide professional development and to assist classroom teachers in delivering reading instruction. Realization of that potential requires that coaches have high levels of knowledge and skills.

The position statement defines the knowledge and skills set necessary. However, at this time the position statement is based heavily on professional wisdom in the absence of solid empirical data.

THE RESEARCH WE NEED

Perhaps the most important need is to have clinical trials that focus on using coaching to improve student achievement. That said, it is not very likely that we will see such studies except perhaps in the evaluations of the Striving Readers Grants funded by the U.S. Department of Education. However, even then we are not likely to be able to evaluate the contribution of coaching to student achievement since curriculum, subject matter area, school contexts, and myriad other factors will vary simultaneously and impact student achievement.

A good starting point for the research effort is developing reliable assessment tools. In the previous section of this chapter, we noted that there is considerable variability in the way coaching is enacted in specific settings. Our first task is to take advantage of this natural variability and use advanced statistical modeling techniques to isolate factors associated with improved student achievement. In order to do that, we must have ways to measure that variability. For example, we know that individual coaches vary along many dimensions: age, experience, level of knowledge about literacy, level of knowledge about subject matter, the amount of time they spend in various activities (e.g., in classroom observation, small-group work, large-group work, planning, assessment), their responsibility for evaluation, whether they work only with teachers or also work with students, and so on. In addition, the teachers and students the coaches work with vary along many similar dimensions. The settings in which coaches work vary by grade level, socioeconomic status, subject matter, coach-to-teacher ratios, the amount of time that coaches spend working with groups of teachers (e.g., in Boston coaches work with teachers in 8-week cycles, while in other cities coaches work with the same group of teachers for an entire academic year or more), sources of funding, instructional materials and strategies that they coach, level of administrative support, and the like. We need solid descriptive work that captures the relevant dimensions of coaching and helps us develop reliable measures of those dimensions. We need to simultaneously have descriptions of setting, coach, teacher, and student behavior, as well as student achievement data.

Figure 8.1 represents one way to conceptualize the complexity of coaching. Ideally we would be able to create assessment tools to help us identify and quantify the critical factors in each of these domains. We could then use statistical modeling techniques to estimate the effects of each of the factors on student reading achievement.

Once we gain some sense of what is critical and develop some strong hypotheses, we can begin to develop more sophisticated studies. My reading of the research literature and interactions with coaches in the field suggests the following factors as potentially powerful determinants of coaching effectiveness:

- Support of school and district administrators
- Interpersonal interaction skills of the coach
- Buy-in from teachers
- Orderly school environment
- Use of data to make instructional decisions
- Access to a variety of interesting and appropriate materials
- Coaches' subject matter knowledge
- Coaches' literacy knowledge

A strong review of the existing case studies and evaluations could help us select some likely hypotheses. In many cases the reports contain interview protocols and occasionally checklists. If we were to develop some strong assessment tools that could be applied across studies and sites, we would make a significant contribution to our understanding of coaching.

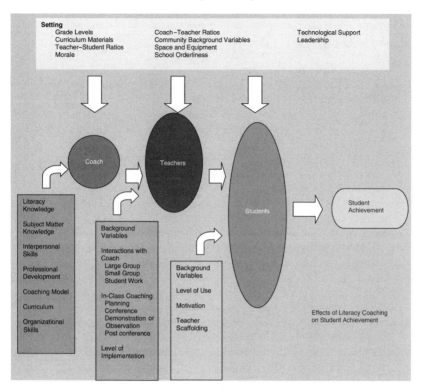

FIGURE 8.1. The complexity of coaching and student achievement.

REFERENCES

Costa, A. L., & Garmston, R. J. (2002). *Cognitive coaching: A foundation for renaissance schools.* Norwood, MA: Christopher-Gordon.

Deford, D., Morgan, D. N., Saylor-Crowder, K. Pae, T., Johnson, R., Stephens, D., et al. (2003). *Changes in children's cue and strategy use during reading: Findings from the first year of professional development in the South Carolina Reading Initiative* (Technical Report No. 002). Columbia: University of South Carolina.

Galm, R., & Perry, G. S., Jr. (2004). Coaching moves beyond the gym. *JSD, 25*(2), 1–4.

Greene, T. (2004). *Literature review for school-based staff developers and coaches.* Oxford, OH: National Staff Development Council. Retrieved October 17, 2006, from *www.nsdc.org/library/schoolbasedlitreview.pdf*

Guskey, T. R. (2000). *Evaluating professional development.* Thousand Oaks, CA: Corwin Press.

International Reading Association. (2004). *The role and qualifications of the reading coach in the United States.* Newark, DE: Author.

International Reading Association. (2006a). *IRA surveys coaches.* Newark, DE: Author.

Retrieved October 16, 2006, from *www.reading.org/publications/reading_today/ samples/RTY-0604–surveys.html*

International Reading Association. (2006b). *Standards for middle and high school literacy coaches.* Newark, DE: Author.

Lyons, C., & Pinnell, G. S. (2001). *Systems for change in literacy education.* Portsmouth, NH: Heinemann.

May, H., Supovitz, J. A., & Lesnick, J. (2004). *The impact of America's choice on writing performance in Georgia: First year results.* College Station, PA: Consortium for Policy Research in Education.

May, H., Supovitz, J. A., & Perda, D. (2004). *A longitudinal study of the impact of America's choice on student performance in Rochester, New York, 1998–2003.* College Station, PA: Consortium for Policy Research in Education.

Neufield, B. N., & Roper, D. (2003). *Coaching: A strategy for developing instructional capacity.* Cambridge, MA: Education Matters, Inc. Retrieved October 16, 2006, from *www.edmatters.org/webreports/Coaching Paperfinal.pdf*

Pearson, P. D., & Gallagher, M. C. (1983). The instruction of reading comprehension. *Contemporary Educational Psychology, 8*(3), 317–344.

Poglinco, S. M., Bach, A. J., Hovde, K., Rosenblum, S., Saunders, M., & Supovitz. J. A. (2003). *The heart of the matter: The coaching model in America's choice schools.* College Station, PA: Consortium for Policy Research in Education.

Richard, A. (2003). *Making our own road.* Denver, CO: Education Commission of the States. Retrieved October 16, 2006, from *www.ecs.org/ html/Document.asp?chouseid =4741*

Rock, H. M. (2002). Job-embedded professional development and reflective coaching. *Instructional Leader, 5*(8), 1–4.

Schwartz, S., & McCarthy, M. (2003). Where the rubber hits the road: An in-depth look at collaborative coaching and learning and workshop instruction in a sample of effective practice schools. In *Boston Plan for Excellence.* Boston: Boston Public Schools.

Snow, C., Ippilito, J., & Schwarz, R. (2006). Section in International Reading Association, *Standards for middle and high school literacy coaches* (pp. 35–49). Newark, DE: International Reading Association.

South Carolina Research Initiative. (2002). *Research on the South Carolina Reading Initiative.* Columbia: University of South Carolina. Retrieved October 16, 2006, from *www.sc.edu/outreach/item.php?oid=14&q= TopicalIndex#reading*

Success for All Foundation. (2006). Research/results. Baltimore: Author. Retrieved October 16, 2006, from *www.successforall.net/research/index.htm*

Supovitz, J. A., & May, H. (2003). *The relationship between teacher implementation of America's Choice and student learning in Plainfield, New Jersey.* College Station, PA: Consortium for Policy Research in Education.

Supovitz, J. A., & Taylor, B. S. (2003). *The impact of standards-based reform in Duval County, Florida: 1999–2002.* College Station, PA: Consortium for Policy Research in Education.

Walpole, S., & McKenna, M. C. (2004). *The literacy's coaches handbook: A guide to research-based practice.* New York: Guilford Press.

West, L., & Staub, F. (2003). *Content-focused coaching: Transforming mathematics lessons.* Portsmouth, NH: Heinemann.

Concluding Reflections

MARK W. CONLEY

In comparison with the entire field of reading research, research on adolescent literacy is in its relative infancy. Going from a preoccupation with teaching techniques in the 1960s, 1970s, and 1980s to an emphasis on understanding adolescents and their multiple literacies in the 1990s, much has been gained with respect to knowing what can be done in classrooms while adolescents engage in many kinds of literate activity. But notice what this leaves out, including what *should be* done and how to help adolescents achieve, particularly those who struggle with literacy learning.

The gap in what we know about what should be done—effective instructional strategies that produce strategic adolescent learners—is particularly poignant at a time like this when the national spotlight is shining on adolescent literacy. Desperate to set some sort of achievable goal, many of the current policies emphasize leading adolescents up to the first year of college. This goal is achievable, but only if we embrace the sometimes complex or expensive options embodied by interventions. But even if we are willing to expend the money or effort, still much more needs to be known about connections between fluency and comprehension, intervention and achievement, or the benefits of additional knowledge and assistance through programs like cognitive coaching.

Even if all of these things are in place, Tatum's Chapter 3 reminds us how we need to know more about what it takes to move adolescents who are isolated and seriously disenfranchised from texts and literacy into successfully literate lives. We do know that positive relationships with adults and peers help; and that teachers' empathy, both cognitive and emotional, is a key; but we know very little about how to ensure that these essential qualities are part of every adolescent's school experience. Moreover, we are only beginning to understand what Moje, in Chapter 4, characterizes as "cultural navigation," the process of helping adolescents expand their everyday knowledge and language into knowledge and facility with academic knowledge and languages. It may be far easier to create and mandate a national test—though not nearly as important—in comparison with making sure that *every* adolescent feels supported rather than alienated from learning.

At a time when the driving force underlying adolescent literacy policy consists of evidence-based practices, we have remarkably little evidence that points us in productive directions. Awkwardly, we have policies in place that enjoy little if any research evidence, such as mandatory literacy courses for secondary teachers. Not that an extra course in literacy is a bad idea, or that research would someday bear out the effectiveness of a literacy course for secondary teachers, but to date there is no clear evidence. And so, at a time when states are adding more literacy courses out of a general idea that somehow this will produce more highly qualified teachers, the research says: We just don't know. As Star, Strickland, and Hawkins suggest in Chapter 6, our gap in understanding key connections between literacy and disciplinary learning, combined with the mandates, creates an urgent need for more research. Tuckey and Anderson's framework for science and literacy, described in Chapter 7, demonstrates just how complex our search for disciplinary connections may be. While literacy researchers have become accustomed to treating the disciplines as monolithic entities, the reality can be more accurately characterized as competing philosophical and epistemological perspectives. It has been easier, from a content-area literacy perspective, to live with the idea of SCIENCE and MATHEMATICS. But, to gain any credibility or validity, adolescent literacy and content-area literacy research needs to embrace the idea that disciplinary learning involves multiple subdisciplines, goals, perspectives, and ultimately literacies.

Clearly, much more research needs to connect adolescents to meaningful futures. Over the past several years, as I observed teachers and their adolescent students, I wondered whether the students have any sense for how the moment in classroom time connects to their past and future lives. I wondered if teachers envision how this topic, this concept, this idea might pay off for their students someday down the road. And if teachers do see that vision, I wondered if they have the time or opportunity to encourage their students to see it. Hopefully, in the future, our work as researchers, teacher educators, teachers, policymakers, and all others concerned with adolescent literacy will help develop this vision while helping teachers and their students make these connections.

Index

Responsive pedagogy
  defined, 59–60
  systemic functional linguistics and,
    73–74
Rhetoric, 71–72

S

San Diego Quick Assessment, 18
School disengagement, African American
    males and, 42
Science
  critical reading skills and, 70
  disciplinary text production and, 71
Science education
  content-oriented critiques, 131–137
  cultural navigation perspective, 75–76,
    77
  prior knowledge activation, 95–96
Science education research
  collaborations between traditions in,
    129–131
  commonplaces/traditions framework,
    116–117, *118*
  content-oriented, 118–122
  discourse-oriented, 118, 125–129
  future directions, 137–140
  strategies-oriented, 118, 122–125
Science learning
  content-oriented perspective on, 121
  discourse-oriented perspective on,
    127–128
  strategies-oriented perspective on,
    124–125
Science teacher education, 138–140
Science teachers
  content-oriented perspective on, 120–
    121
  discourse-oriented perspective on, 127
  strategies-oriented perspective on, 123,
    124
Science texts
  content-oriented perspective on, 119,
    120, 132–137
  discourse-oriented perspective on, 126,
    127
  possible research areas on, 140
  science writing heuristic and, 71
  strategies-oriented perspective on,
    123–124
Science writing heuristic (SWH), 71
Scientific application, 135

Scientific arguments and practices, 133–
    135
Scientific data, 133–134
Scientific inquiry, 119–120, 135
Scientific literacy
  content-oriented perspective on, 121
  definitions of, 113–114, 115
  discourse-oriented perspective on, 128
  features of, 65
  fictionalized situation illustrating
    questions in, 115–116
  strategies-oriented perspective on, 125
Scientific models and theories, 134–135
Scientific observations, 133–134
Screening tests, 16, 23–24
Silent reading comprehension, 5–6
Social context, African American males
    and, 41
Statewide reading assessments, 16
Strategic comprehension knowledge, 22–23
Strategic decoding, 20
Strategic fluency, 21
Strategic instruction model (SIM), 122
Strategic questions, 94
Strategic vocabulary knowledge, 21–22
Strategies-oriented research, 118, 122–
    125, 129–131
Strategy instruction
  developing comprehension knowledge,
    22–23
  developing decoding, 20
  developing fluency, 21
  developing vocabulary knowledge, 21–
    22
  principles of, 20
Striving Readers Grants, 148
Struggling adolescent readers, 14–15, 91–
    93, 99
Student achievement, literacy coaching
    and, *151*
Student agency, 115
Student learning in science
  content-oriented perspective on, 121
  discourse-oriented perspective on,
    127–128
  strategies-oriented perspective on,
    124–125
Student–technology interactions, 96–98
Subject-area study, 15
Sustained Silent Reading (SSR), 5
Systemic functional linguistics, 73–75